(Chapter One)

(Rise Up)

It all started in a little small town in Norwood Ohio. The year was 1972 and at that time the small town was flourishing only because of addition of the General Motors Company had placed its roots and made it their home. Manufacturing their many styles of cars from the Norwood plant.

The summers were filled with very much fun. There was a lot to do. Swimming and playing baseball and football and basketball as well. Chasing the girls back in those days was also the young men's favorite thing to do most of all. There was a group of about 8 young men who all hung out together.

They hung out almost every single day together. Swimming at the local pool. Or heading out to the several swings at the rivers they'd known about. Some days they would head all the way out to East Fork left. Not only to swim but to check out all of the pretty girls who would also be out at the lake.

Back then the lakes in Ohio were the local hotspots. That and the Skating rinks that were in locations spread about the Cincinnati area as well. Then the drinking and partying would start shortly after Jeffrey's 15th birthday. He would quickly turn into a wild young man.

Their wasn't anything that he wouldn't try atleast once. Whether it was safe or not he was always one of the first to give it a go. Whether it be a cliff dive from up high or a dare to swim across the local gravel pits in Newtown. Or even the Little Miami River or thee Ohio River for that matter.

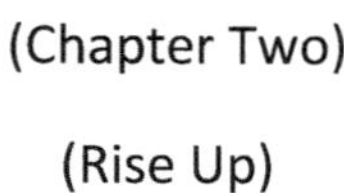

## (Chapter Two)

## (Rise Up)

Jeffrey was a dare devil. He didn't know and for the life of him couldn't figure out just in the hell where this witness came from within him. His twin brother passing  away just after birth had affected him greatly once he was old enough to find out and really understand what had happened that day.

.

After his parents had told him the truth about the story of his brothers passing Jeffrey was completely torn apart by the facts. From that moment forward it would directly affect his life for the worst for very many years. On his birthday's a deep state of depression would set in on him.

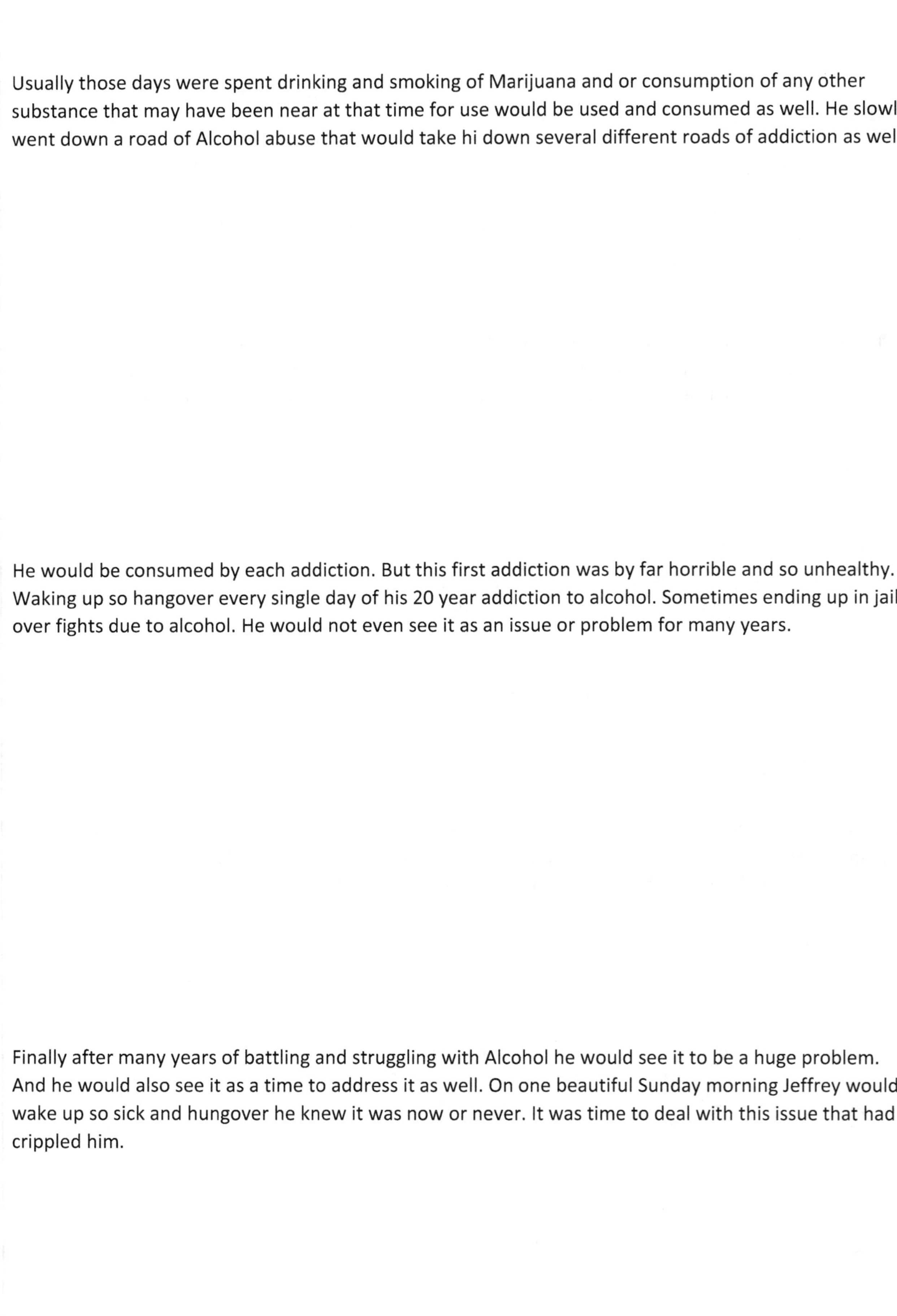

Usually those days were spent drinking and smoking of Marijuana and or consumption of any other substance that may have been near at that time for use would be used and consumed as well. He slowly went down a road of Alcohol abuse that would take hi down several different roads of addiction as well.

He would be consumed by each addiction. But this first addiction was by far horrible and so unhealthy. Waking up so hangover every single day of his 20 year addiction to alcohol. Sometimes ending up in jail over fights due to alcohol. He would not even see it as an issue or problem for many years.

Finally after many years of battling and struggling with Alcohol he would see it to be a huge problem. And he would also see it as a time to address it as well. On one beautiful Sunday morning Jeffrey would wake up so sick and hungover he knew it was now or never. It was time to deal with this issue that had crippled him.

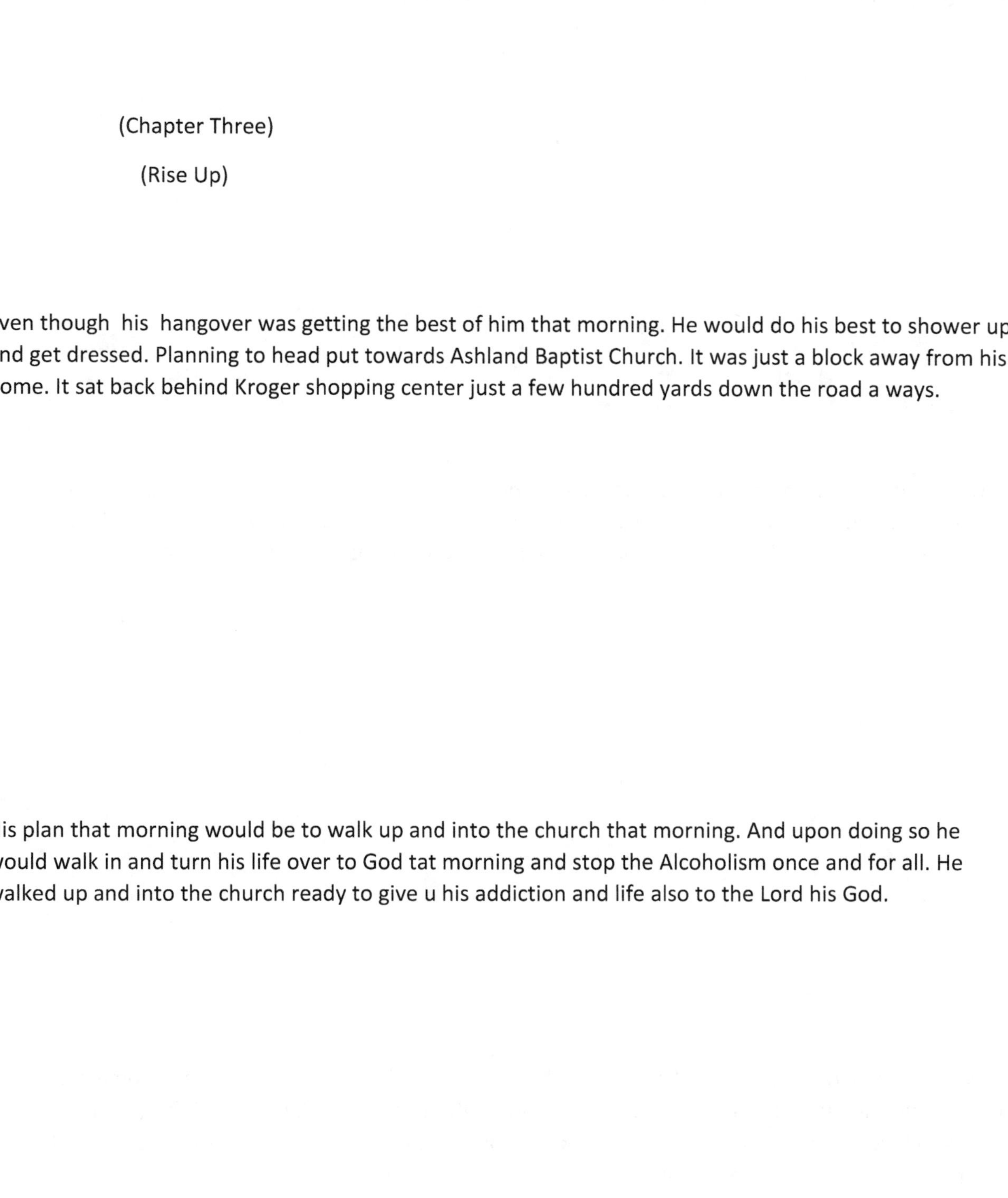

(Chapter Three)

(Rise Up)

Even though  his  hangover was getting the best of him that morning. He would do his best to shower up and get dressed. Planning to head put towards Ashland Baptist Church. It was just a block away from his home. It sat back behind Kroger shopping center just a few hundred yards down the road a ways.

His plan that morning would be to walk up and into the church that morning. And upon doing so he would walk in and turn his life over to God tat morning and stop the Alcoholism once and for all. He walked up and into the church ready to give u his addiction and life also to the Lord his God.

He walked into the church and asked the fellow brothers of the church to help him that morning he wanted to be cleansed of all of his sins and turn his life over to the lord once and for all. He was ready to live a different life from that moment forward. His life to that point had been a total train wreck.

Pure hell was his day in and day out routine for very many years. From back when he was a child being tortured and traumatized by other family members for years. His father was an alcoholic and his father before him was also an Alcoholic as well. The Addiction pattern was fully set in place in the Lilly families blood line.

He had remembered back to the days of his father and fathers friends and his uncles all come home nightly drunk and staggering through the door being highly intoxicated. Even once Jeffrey was accidentally set on fire by his drunk uncle Jack coming in one night so drunkard intoxicated he had dropped his cigar onto Jeffrey's blanket.

Quickly setting it on fire and burning Jeffrey's fingers and toes very badly. So badly he would miss school for several days due to the pain from the burns he had suffered from the accident that had taken place that night. All the women of the family tried to comfort Jeffrey from the pain he was suffering from.

## (Chapter Four)

## (Rise Up)

As he was being dressed and ready for his baptism directly in the back room behind the church alter where the priest was giving his current sermon on that beautiful Sunday during the long and very hot dog days of that late July in 1997. His whole life flashed before his eyes during his baptism. And in the snap of a finger it was all over and done.

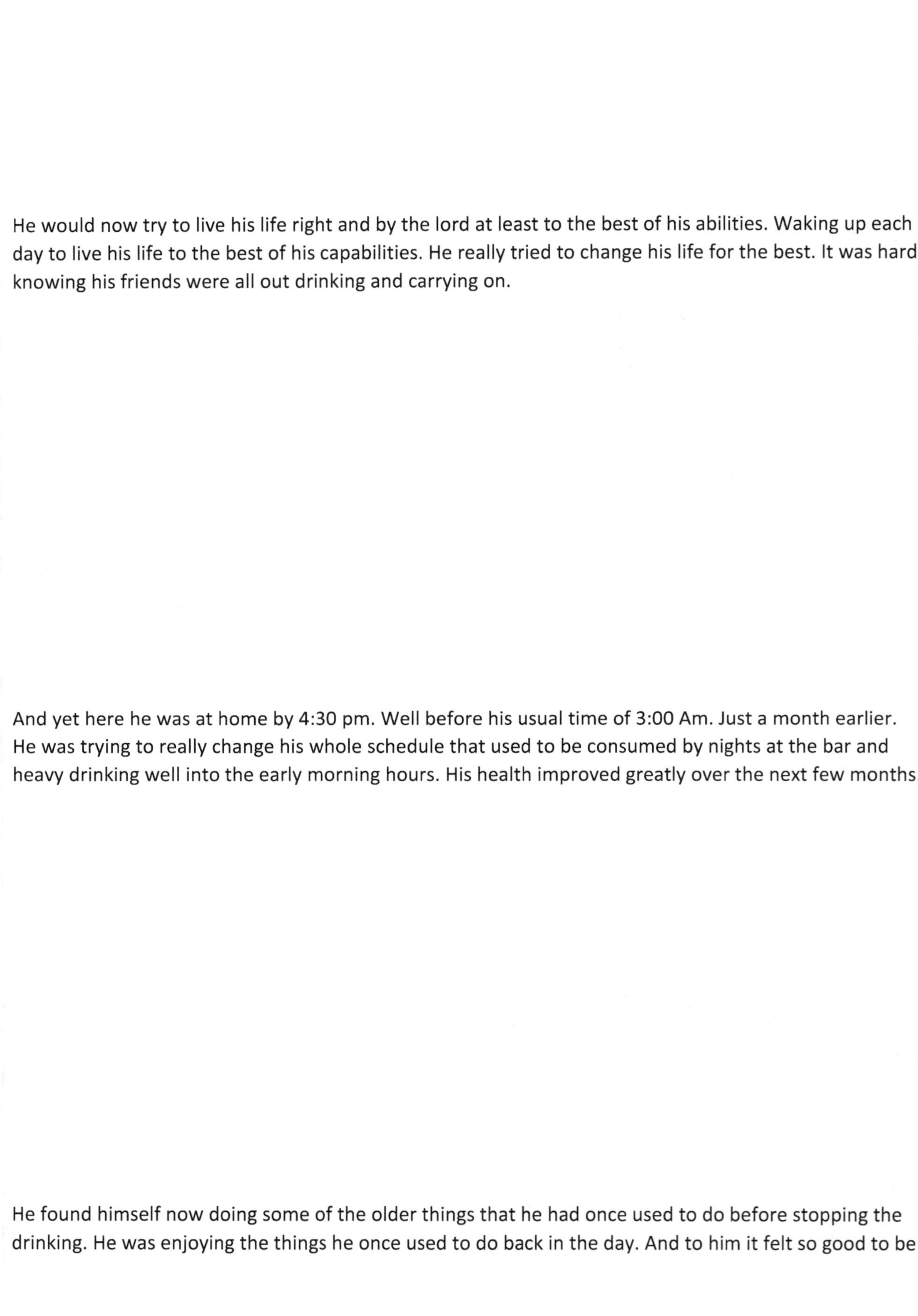

He would now try to live his life right and by the lord at least to the best of his abilities. Waking up each day to live his life to the best of his capabilities. He really tried to change his life for the best. It was hard knowing his friends were all out drinking and carrying on.

And yet here he was at home by 4:30 pm. Well before his usual time of 3:00 Am. Just a month earlier. He was trying to really change his whole schedule that used to be consumed by nights at the bar and heavy drinking well into the early morning hours. His health improved greatly over the next few months.

He found himself now doing some of the older things that he had once used to do before stopping the drinking. He was enjoying the things he once used to do back in the day. And to him it felt so good to be

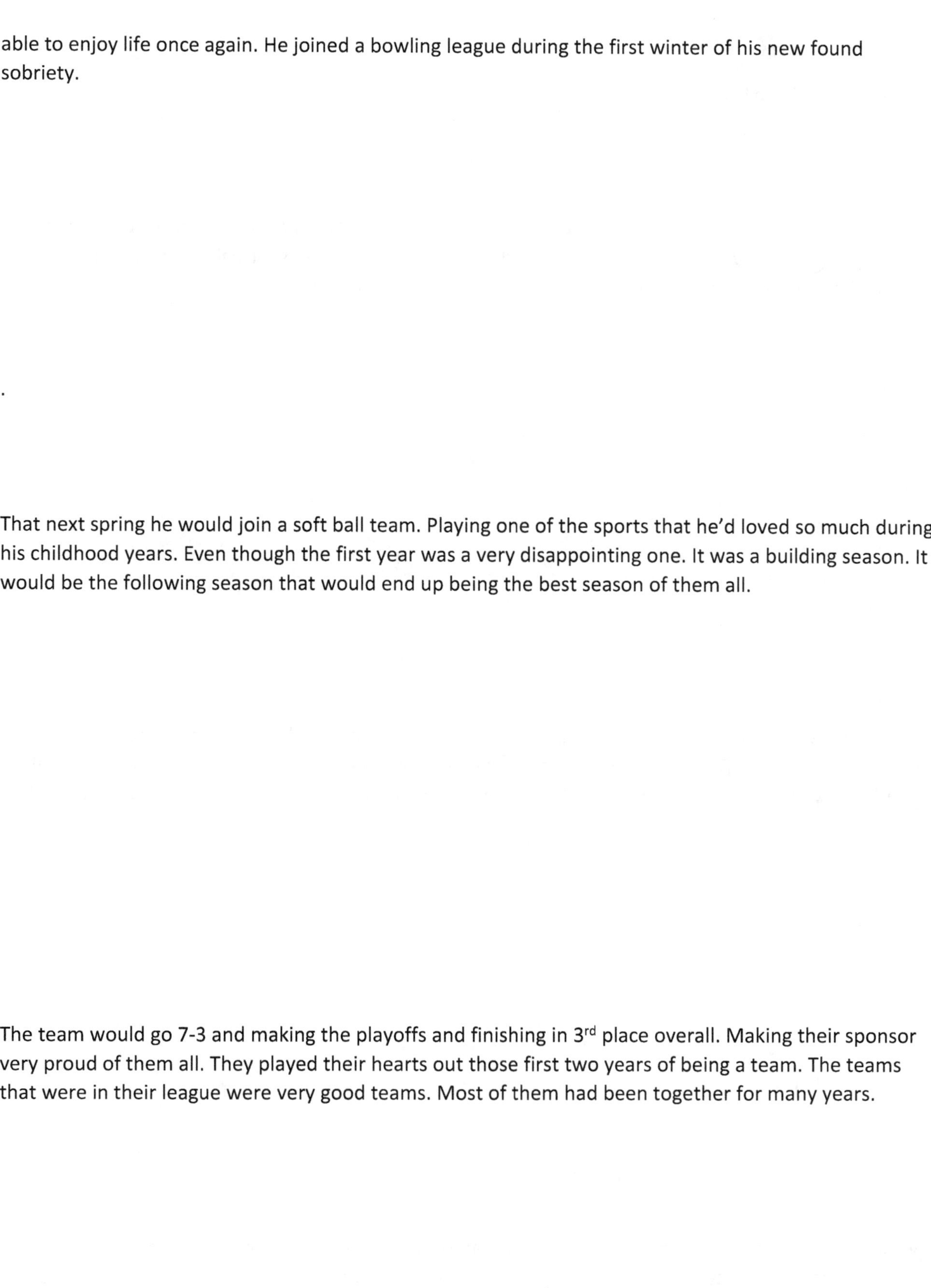

able to enjoy life once again. He joined a bowling league during the first winter of his new found sobriety.

That next spring he would join a soft ball team. Playing one of the sports that he'd loved so much during his childhood years. Even though the first year was a very disappointing one. It was a building season. It would be the following season that would end up being the best season of them all.

The team would go 7-3 and making the playoffs and finishing in 3rd place overall. Making their sponsor very proud of them all. They played their hearts out those first two years of being a team. The teams that were in their league were very good teams. Most of them had been together for many years.

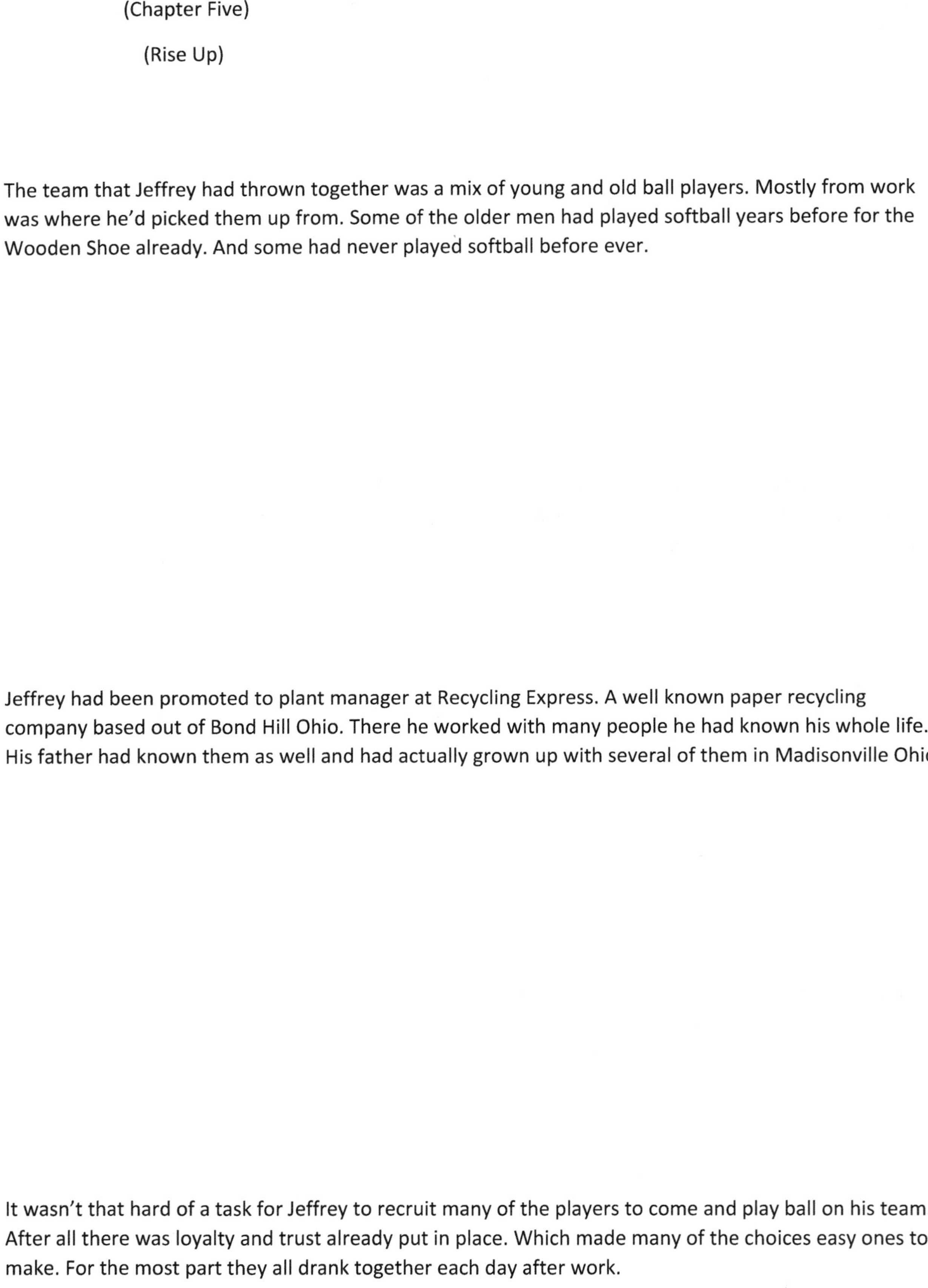

## (Chapter Five)

## (Rise Up)

The team that Jeffrey had thrown together was a mix of young and old ball players. Mostly from work was where he'd picked them up from. Some of the older men had played softball years before for the Wooden Shoe already. And some had never played softball before ever.

Jeffrey had been promoted to plant manager at Recycling Express. A well known paper recycling company based out of Bond Hill Ohio. There he worked with many people he had known his whole life. His father had known them as well and had actually grown up with several of them in Madisonville Ohio.

It wasn't that hard of a task for Jeffrey to recruit many of the players to come and play ball on his team. After all there was loyalty and trust already put in place. Which made many of the choices easy ones to make. For the most part they all drank together each day after work.

So the plan was to take their weekends to practice down at the local baseball fields at Water Works Park. Lower Norwood Ohio being the location. If those fields were taken at the time they would take the team down even lower to upper Mill crest park. Or Lower Mill crest Park.

Both parks were good baseball fields that would give the team the ample time that they needed to become an even better team. They practiced many weekend's to keep their rhythm together. And to keep their batting skills up to par before the next game would take place. Wednesdays was Game Day. It was marked on each of the players schedules.

Everyone always showed up early usually either at the bar or at Water Works One baseball diamond which was down the hill from Water Works pool. The teams that were on this current list were made up of some very good ball players. Some players were just phenomenal ball players.

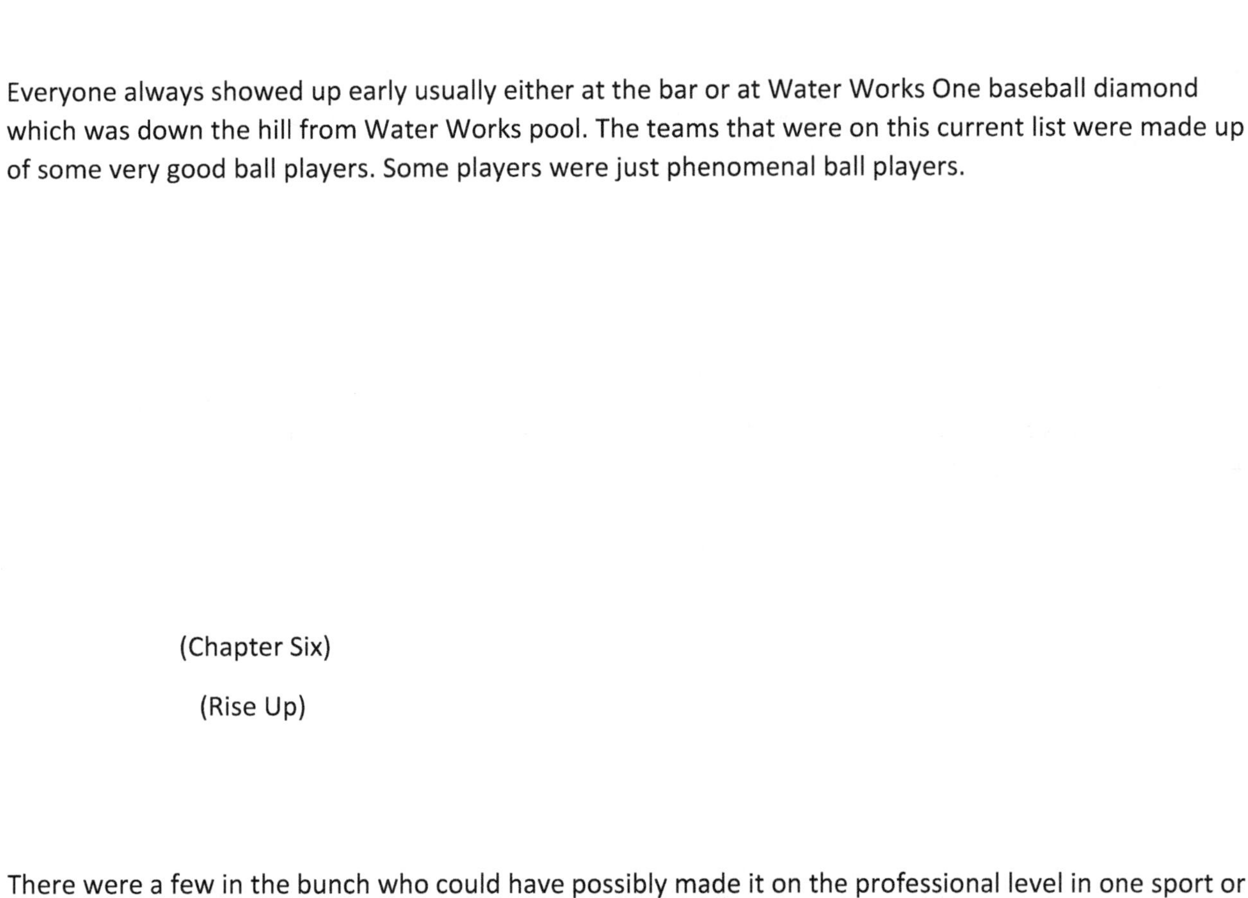

## (Chapter Six)

## (Rise Up)

There were a few in the bunch who could have possibly made it on the professional level in one sport or another. There was quite a bit of talent that had came out of Norwood Ohio. But there had been a ton of talent lost by bad decision making as well. And that was one thing that was for sure.

Alcohol and Drugs and women chasing had led to a lot of young men losing out on their fate in the sports world. Now most Wednesdays were spent re living dreams. And pretending they were in the big leagues while out on the field. Hot dogging and show boating went on a lot.

At least now Jeffrey had been clean from the Alcoholism after 20 years of being dog drunk every single day of his life. He was now trying to live his life as normal as possible. He was working everyday and going home and being a father to his son. To the best of his abilities any way he could he tried to improve himself as a man.

But then after having a freak accident just before a ball game back in his youth. Jeffrey would again have rising issues with his mouth over that accident. One day while at work he would pass out straight on the floor in the middle of a shift. Waking up at the hospital with pain in his mouth and a swollen face.

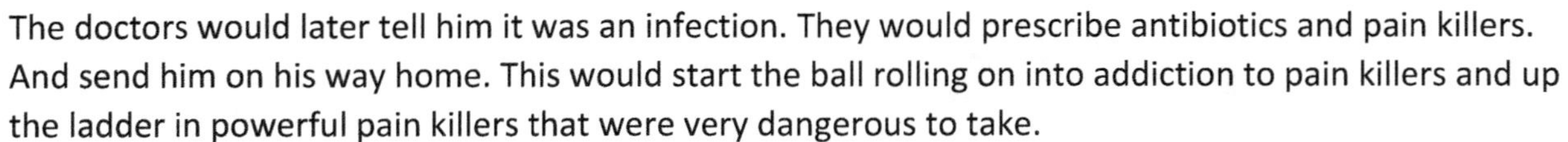

The doctors would later tell him it was an infection. They would prescribe antibiotics and pain killers. And send him on his way home. This would start the ball rolling on into addiction to pain killers and up the ladder in powerful pain killers that were very dangerous to take.

## (Chapter Seven)

## (Rise Up)

Jeff would slowly start taking Vicodin for pain and graduate on up to the extra strength Vicodin 750 milligram pills. And on into the world of Percocet. Starting with the good ones the  Endocets was their nickname. They would kill the pain and give a high like no other. But as with all drugs the body begins to become immune to them over time.

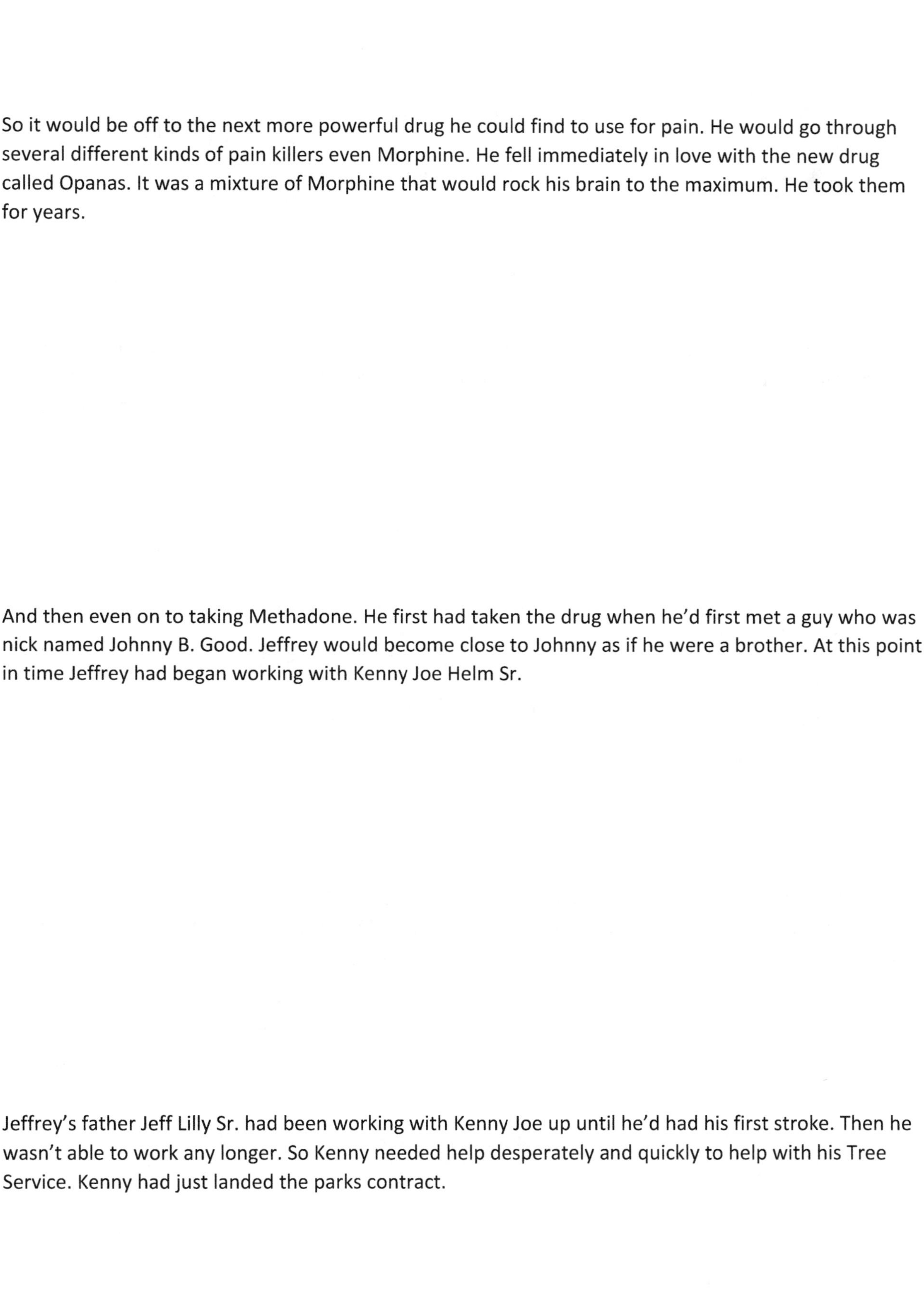

So it would be off to the next more powerful drug he could find to use for pain. He would go through several different kinds of pain killers even Morphine. He fell immediately in love with the new drug called Opanas. It was a mixture of Morphine that would rock his brain to the maximum. He took them for years.

And then even on to taking Methadone. He first had taken the drug when he'd first met a guy who was nick named Johnny B. Good. Jeffrey would become close to Johnny as if he were a brother. At this point in time Jeffrey had began working with Kenny Joe Helm Sr.

Jeffrey's father Jeff Lilly Sr. had been working with Kenny Joe up until he'd had his first stroke. Then he wasn't able to work any longer. So Kenny needed help desperately and quickly to help with his Tree Service. Kenny had just landed the parks contract.

So Jeffrey Jr. had decided to go to work for and help Kenny out of his jam. He worked so hard for the company. Often crawling in the front door of the house suffering from pure exhaustion from working out in the sun and the heat all day. But he would make it and end up working with Kenny for years.

## (Chapter Eight)

## (Rise Up)

The crew had hit it off as a whole unit. Working very well together. Which in return impressed the council members of the City of Norwood landing Kenny Joe and his crew the parks tree contract. That ensured the crew a permanent job with the signing of that contract.

They would have other jobs in other towns across Cincinnati that they would have to do as well. But for the most part the parks would be their new bread and butter. They would stay busy for the next ten years until Kenny developed cancer. The cancer had came in out of nowhere and took Kenny out in no time at all.

He suffered badly in the end. Not being able to even take his pain meds on his own. It was a sad time in all of our lives. The man that we had grown to love and work with was now going to die from a terrible cancer. Pancreatic cancer a horrible disease in which would cause a great deal of pain at the end.

After Kenny passed away we were all hurting bad deeply inside our souls. Not only had addiction been taking our loved ones away early in life. But death from other illnesses had been stripping our small town of all of the people Jeffrey had known and had grown up with.

Jeffrey had taken all of the deaths so hard he had beaten Alcohol addiction only to fall victim to yet another addiction one after another it seemed. Now it was pain pills that had the monkey on his back so to speak. This wouldn't be a battle that would be overcame quickly. Jeffrey would suffer for a long period of time before seeing the light.

## (Chapter Nine)

## (Rise Up)

The struggle was real as it could get for him. Day in and day out it was a battle. One day being a good day another being a bad day. Jobs would be hard to come by. Now that Kenny was gone nobody wanted to hire Jeffrey because of his record. A Felony one Felony Child Support conviction had crushed many great job opportunities.

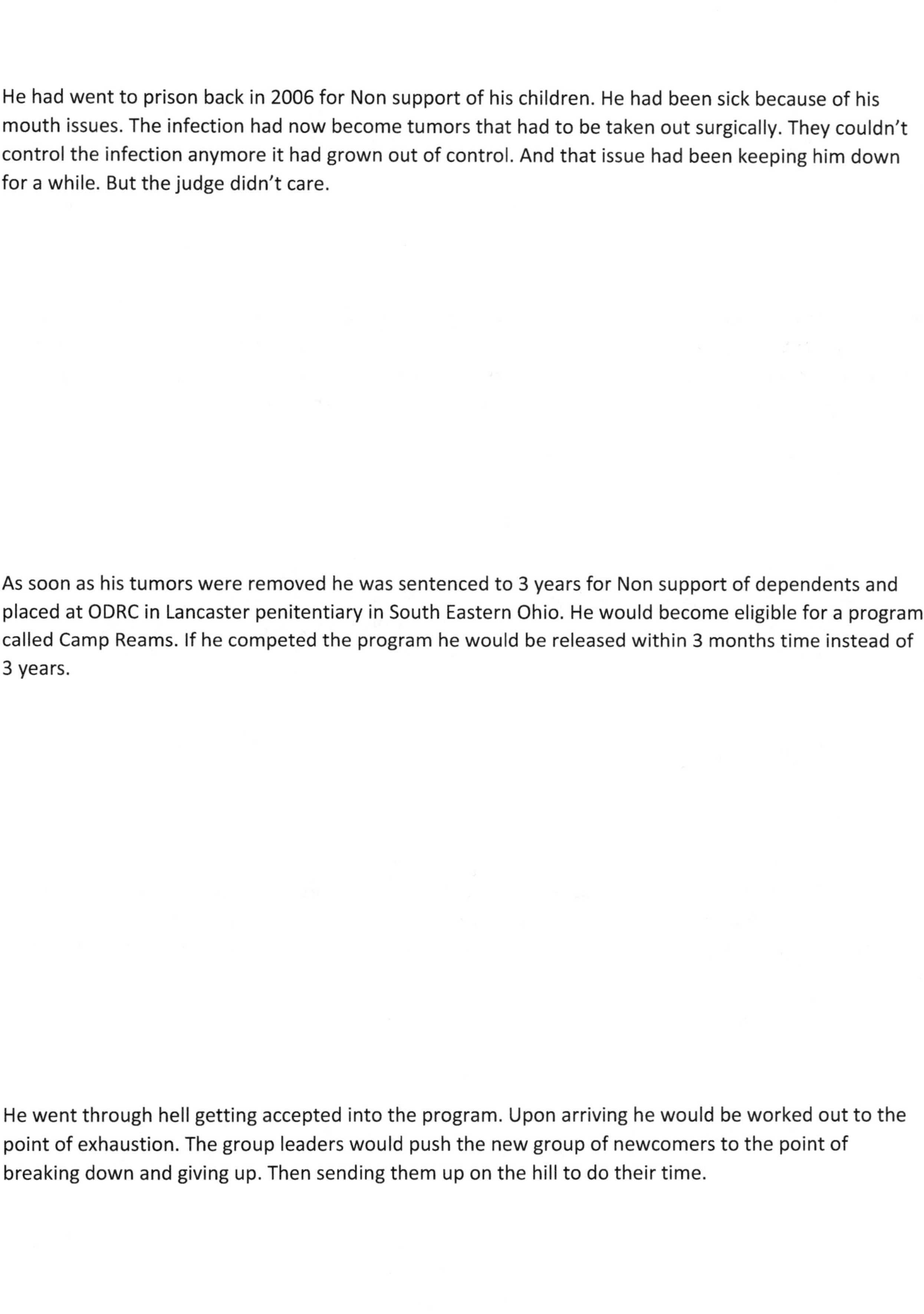

He had went to prison back in 2006 for Non support of his children. He had been sick because of his mouth issues. The infection had now become tumors that had to be taken out surgically. They couldn't control the infection anymore it had grown out of control. And that issue had been keeping him down for a while. But the judge didn't care.

As soon as his tumors were removed he was sentenced to 3 years for Non support of dependents and placed at ODRC in Lancaster penitentiary in South Eastern Ohio. He would become eligible for a program called Camp Reams. If he competed the program he would be released within 3 months time instead of 3 years.

He went through hell getting accepted into the program. Upon arriving he would be worked out to the point of exhaustion. The group leaders would push the new group of newcomers to the point of breaking down and giving up. Then sending them up on the hill to do their time.

Jeffrey would get up each morning at 5 Am shower up eat breakfast then workout for an hour. Then go to work on the chain gang for 6 to 8 hours and then back to camp for dinner and school and even more workouts. It seemed that the leaders of the camp were all ex military. And wouldn't put us through anything that they couldn't do and worked out with us each and every time.

## (Chapter Ten)

## (Rise Up)

It would be in the dead of winter Lancaster Ohio. Just south of Columbus. 6 inches of fresh snow outside and at 6 am we would go on a run shortly after breakfast. 5 miles out and 5 miles back. In the snow up and down hills and valleys. Bear country as well. Some of the runs I have to say were very scary to me.

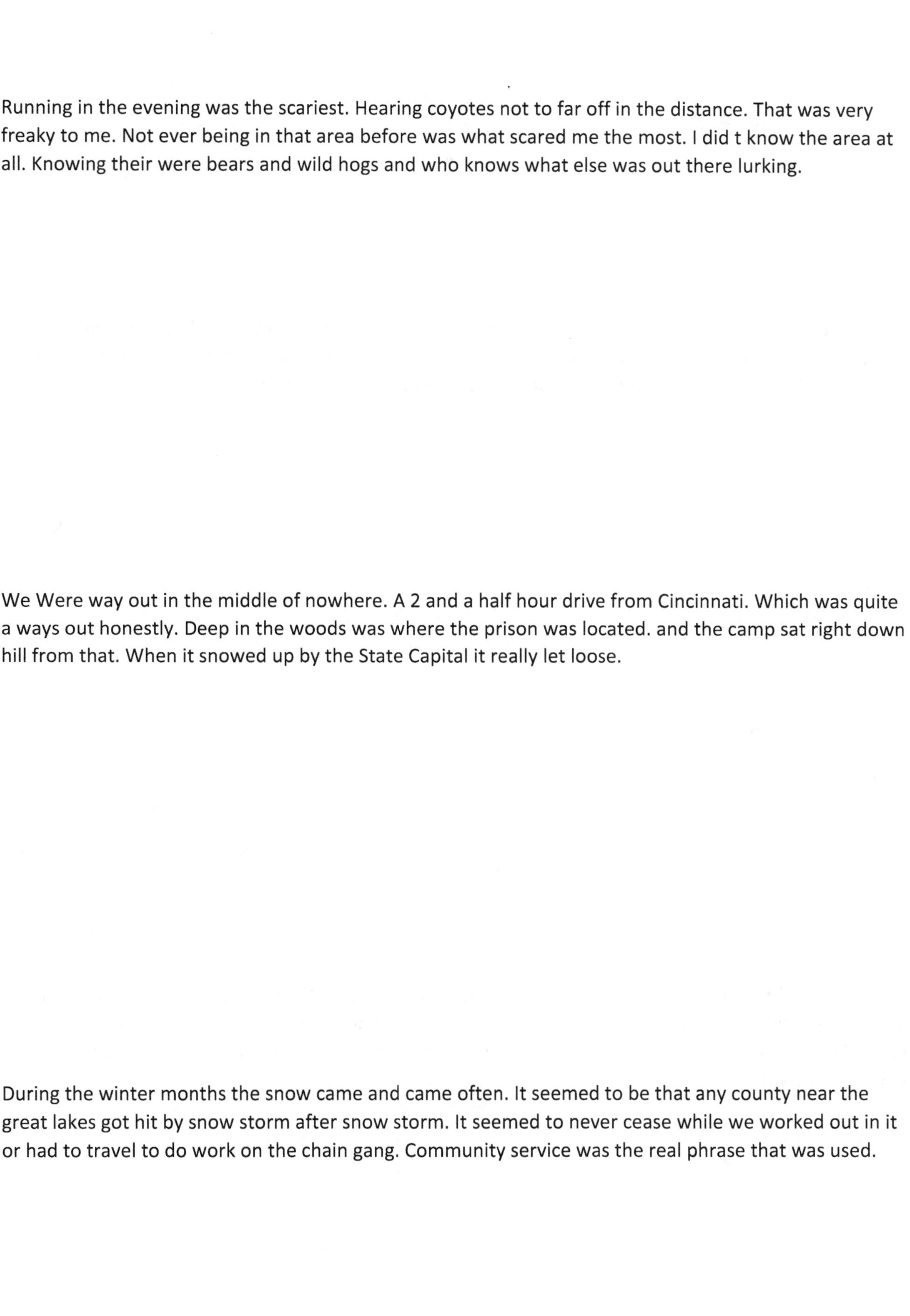

Running in the evening was the scariest. Hearing coyotes not to far off in the distance. That was very freaky to me. Not ever being in that area before was what scared me the most. I did t know the area at all. Knowing their were bears and wild hogs and who knows what else was out there lurking.

We Were way out in the middle of nowhere. A 2 and a half hour drive from Cincinnati. Which was quite a ways out honestly. Deep in the woods was where the prison was located. and the camp sat right down hill from that. When it snowed up by the State Capital it really let loose.

During the winter months the snow came and came often. It seemed to be that any county near the great lakes got hit by snow storm after snow storm. It seemed to never cease while we worked out in it or had to travel to do work on the chain gang. Community service was the real phrase that was used.

We worked hard every day in the cold all day then would have to come back and shower up for school and then eat workout once again and then head off for school. The evenings after school was our free time. Wasn't much but it was ours. We would usually watch television or work out even more.

## (Chapter Eleven)

## (Rise Up)

It was a setup just like the Military without weapons that was about the description. The grind day in and day out. But after 90 days of that I actually graduated the program. Passed the pre general education test as well with the Time I'd spent wisely. I went in to the program knowing in my soul I wouldn't allow myself to fail.

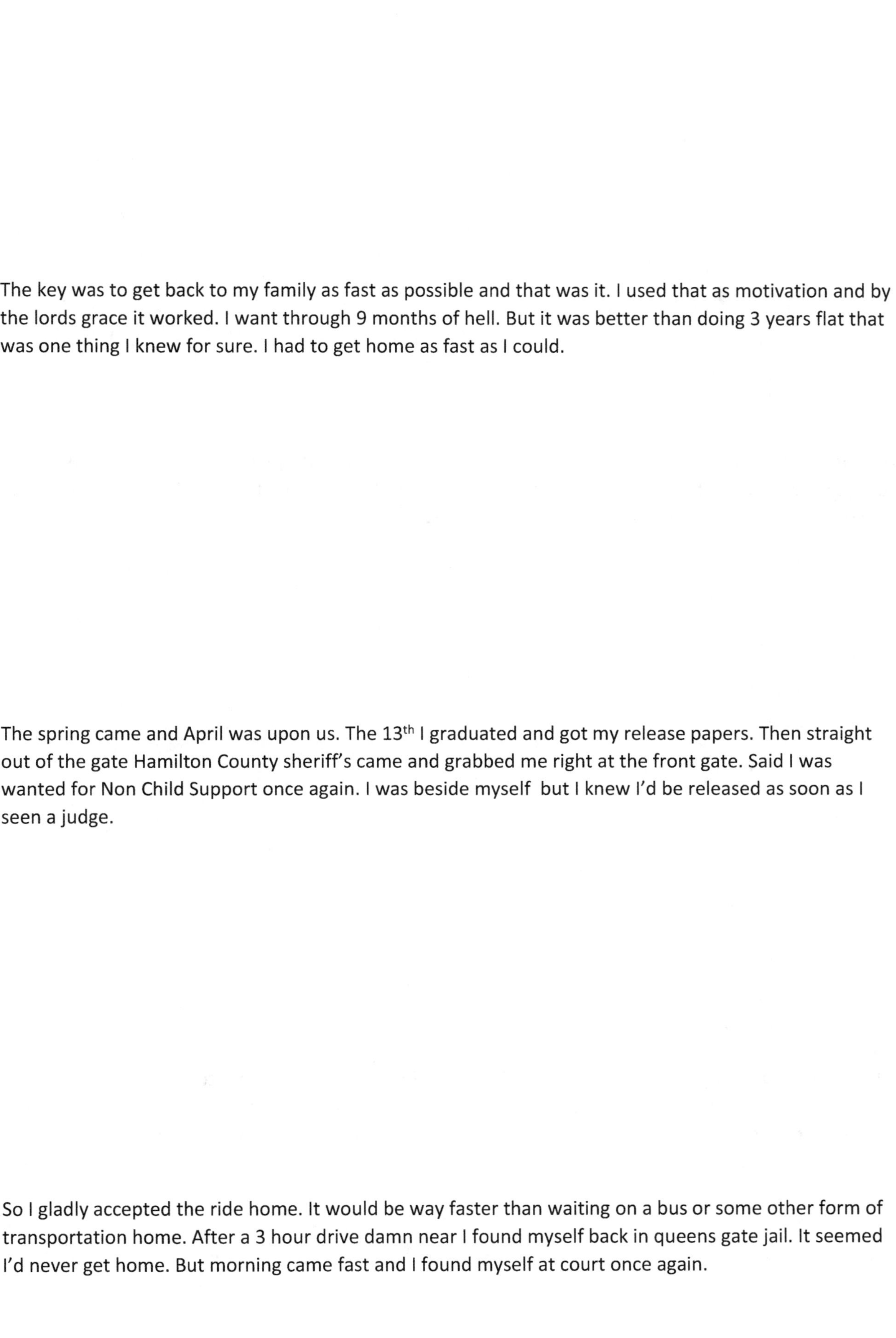

The key was to get back to my family as fast as possible and that was it. I used that as motivation and by the lords grace it worked. I want through 9 months of hell. But it was better than doing 3 years flat that was one thing I knew for sure. I had to get home as fast as I could.

The spring came and April was upon us. The $13^{th}$ I graduated and got my release papers. Then straight out of the gate Hamilton County sheriff's came and grabbed me right at the front gate. Said I was wanted for Non Child Support once again. I was beside myself but I knew I'd be released as soon as I seen a judge.

So I gladly accepted the ride home. It would be way faster than waiting on a bus or some other form of transportation home. After a 3 hour drive damn near I found myself back in queens gate jail. It seemed I'd never get home. But morning came fast and I found myself at court once again.

They asked me where I had been and I quickly told them prison and they had sent me their. I was released shortly after that and got to go home finally after all the hell and torment I'd suffered over the 10 months of brutal weather and exhausting workouts.

## (Chapter Twelve)

## (Rise Up)

When I hit the door my Sister Joanne and her Boyfriend Brad Carter were there to pick me up and take me home. I remember that I was so afraid that I'd lose a family member before I got home. That was the one thing I feared the most of all. I was so grateful that I didn't lose anyone on this trip up state.

When I arrived home I was excited as could be. Before I could hit the front door I was picked up by Scotty Rodgers. We took off for the bar as soon as I hit the threshold it was a wrap. I was wasted before 6 o'clock pm. But we partied on until past the midnight hour.

I got home shortly after 2:45 in the morning. Drunker than 5 people put together. I didn't expect that ordeal to even happen. But it did and my first night I also used for the first time again. I bought an oxy 40 MG from an old high-school friend of mine while at the good old Lutche's Café Norwood Ohio.

I woke up so hungover it was crazy. To go out and get crazy drunk my first night out of prison. But he'll I had no family with me they had all left and went down home to Virginia on me while I was away. They would come home as soon as they had heard news of me being home once again.

I spent the 2nd day home with my family that day was cool. It felt so comfortable to be with family once again finally. I had missed my Mother and Father very much so. I hadn't made one call home to tell them I was OK while I was away from home in jail.

## (Chapter Thirteen)

## (Rise Up)

I was so damn afraid that I would lose my father while I was away. He had been in such bad shape while I was away. At any moment he could pass away. Which was the only thing that I really feared for the most part. Mom was OK she had been thru some sickness here and there but for the most part she had remained the strong woman.

She was my Rock and My Shield that woman. I loved having her as one of  my best friends. She would be good enough to make it. But she would get sick years later. I was home now that's all that mattered to me at this point in time. Life would move forward and addictions would kick in yet again.

I couldn't seem to get the monkey off of my back. No matter how hard I tried to get sober. Something was holding me back from being free from deep within. Years down the rad it would all play out and I would become sober finally. But after losing so many things in life. Nothing but simple possessions.

It wasn't the loss of possessions that got the best of me. It was the loss of my self control that really got me. I had lost my balance in life. All the way ten fold. I didn't know in which way to turn or go for help. All of my friends and loved ones were dying all around me.

It wasn't until I had lost a close and dear friend. Greg Petrie that I would really get it for what it was. Addiction that was. A life or death battle that had taken so many loved ones away very early in their lives. I was a lost soul at this point. I called a local rehabilitation program on December 23rd of 2015 and was told to hold on until the 26th.

## (Chapter Fourteen)

## (Rise Up)

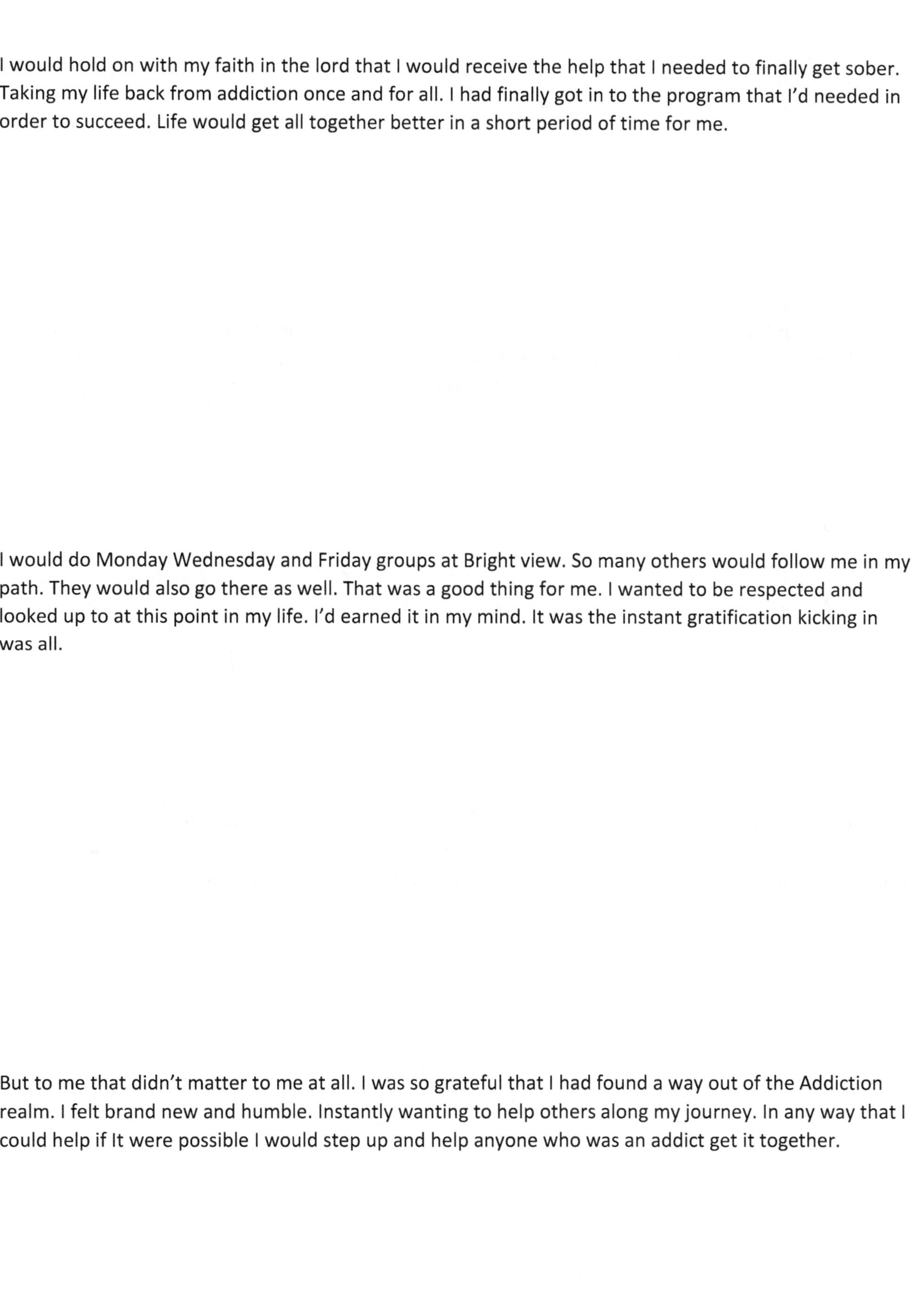

I would hold on with my faith in the lord that I would receive the help that I needed to finally get sober. Taking my life back from addiction once and for all. I had finally got in to the program that I'd needed in order to succeed. Life would get all together better in a short period of time for me.

I would do Monday Wednesday and Friday groups at Bright view. So many others would follow me in my path. They would also go there as well. That was a good thing for me. I wanted to be respected and looked up to at this point in my life. I'd earned it in my mind. It was the instant gratification kicking in was all.

But to me that didn't matter to me at all. I was so grateful that I had found a way out of the Addiction realm. I felt brand new and humble. Instantly wanting to help others along my journey. In any way that I could help if It were possible I would step up and help anyone who was an addict get it together.

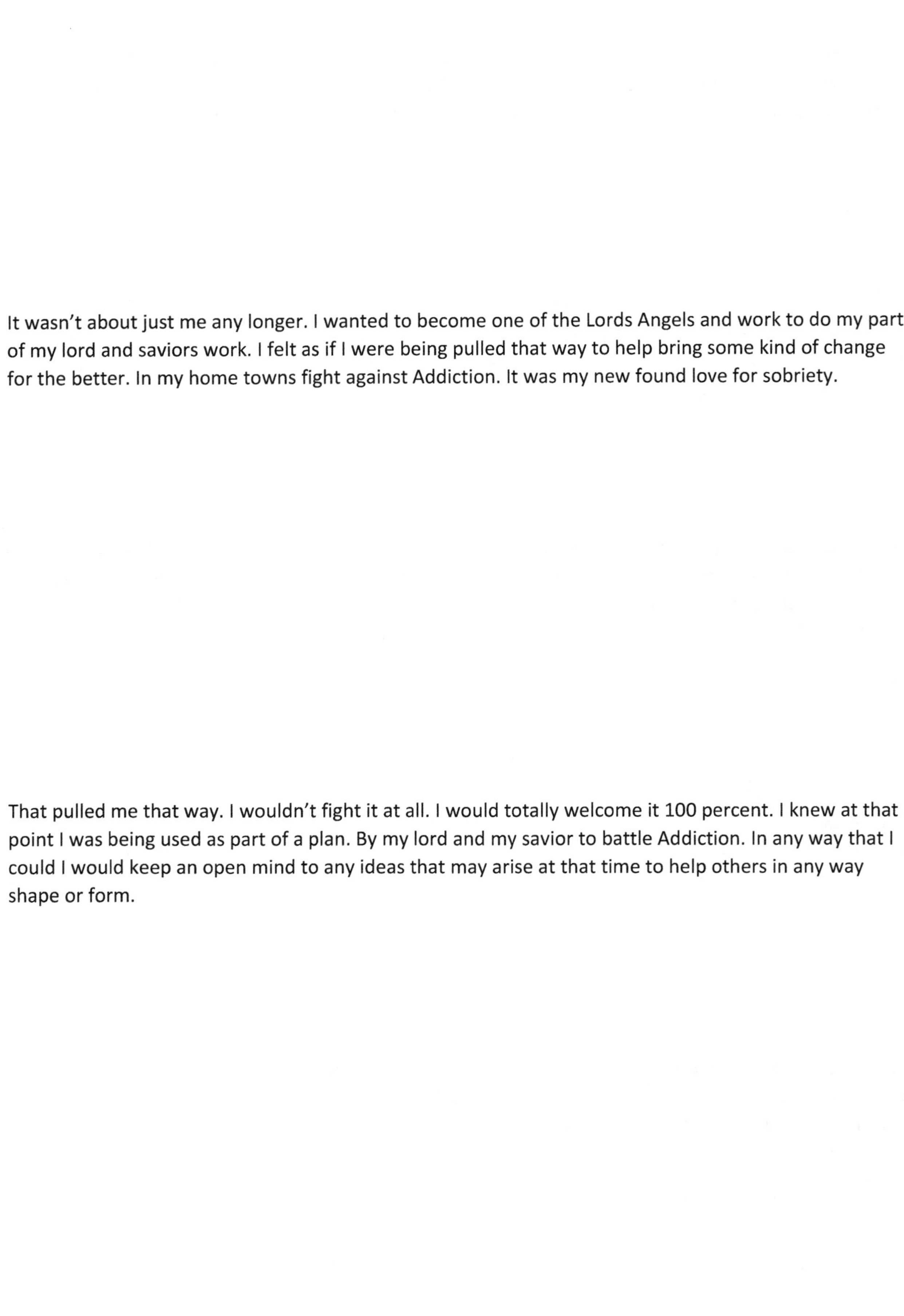

It wasn’t about just me any longer. I wanted to become one of the Lords Angels and work to do my part of my lord and saviors work. I felt as if I were being pulled that way to help bring some kind of change for the better. In my home towns fight against Addiction. It was my new found love for sobriety.

That pulled me that way. I wouldn’t fight it at all. I would totally welcome it 100 percent. I knew at that point I was being used as part of a plan. By my lord and my savior to battle Addiction. In any way that I could I would keep an open mind to any ideas that may arise at that time to help others in any way shape or form.

It would work eventually. I would find my way through the battle and take several others with me along the way. Now having started to put a dent in the numbers toward a positive direction in my hometown. There had become a new energy and vibe in the air. People had started to help each other once again.

## (Chapter Fifteen)

## (Rise Up)

It seemed that we had taken back power over the Addiction that was slowly consuming our small town. The battle had begun and for once we were winning. The number of addicts that we'd once had were starting to lower. And for all of us that had become a new found happiness. A new Joy overwhelmed us all.

We had learned how to work as a team. And we were at this point in our zone our new found groove. And that feeling would last for quite a while. We were in the battle together now and winning the war

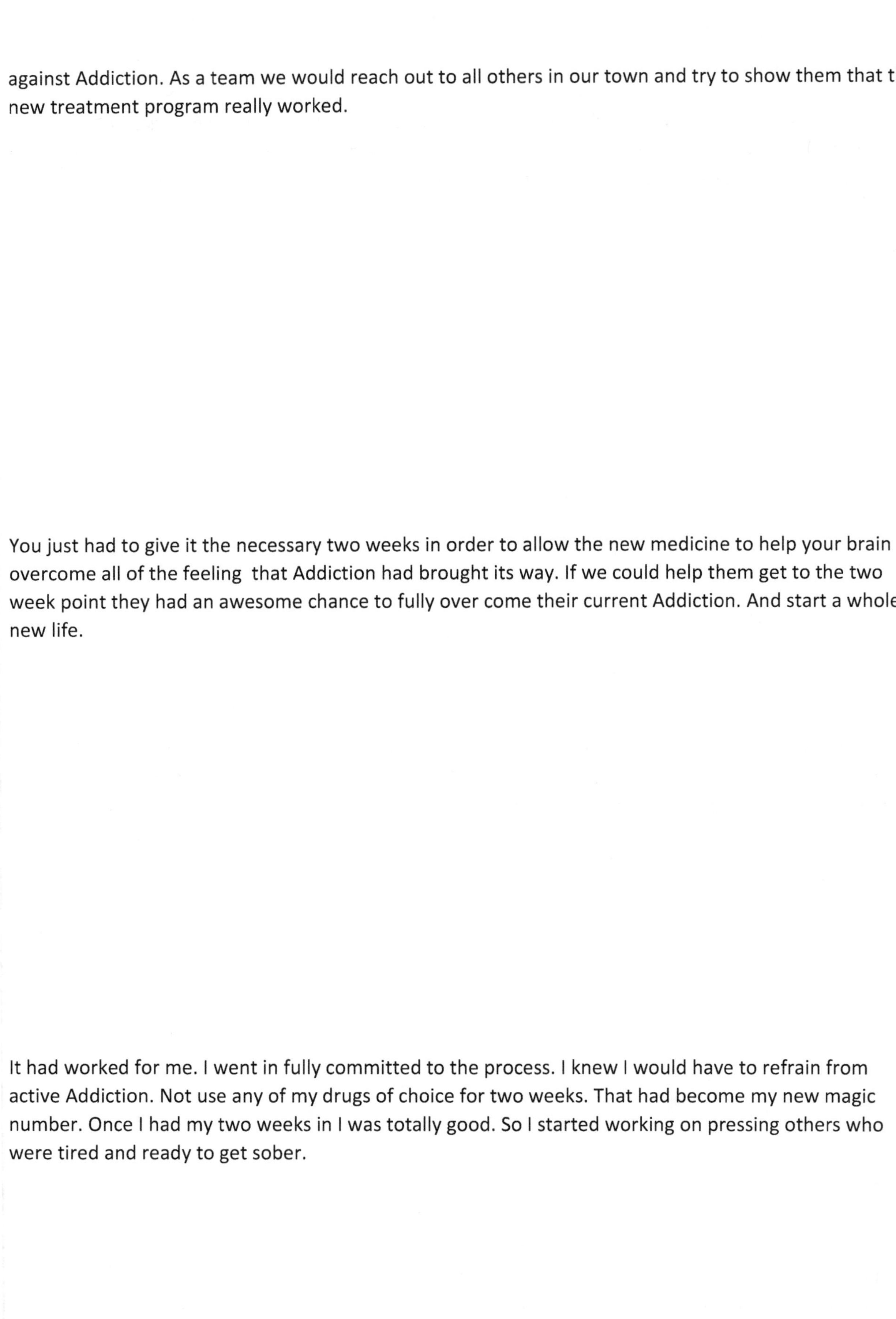

against Addiction. As a team we would reach out to all others in our town and try to show them that this new treatment program really worked.

You just had to give it the necessary two weeks in order to allow the new medicine to help your brain overcome all of the feeling that Addiction had brought its way. If we could help them get to the two week point they had an awesome chance to fully over come their current Addiction. And start a whole new life.

It had worked for me. I went in fully committed to the process. I knew I would have to refrain from active Addiction. Not use any of my drugs of choice for two weeks. That had become my new magic number. Once I had my two weeks in I was totally good. So I started working on pressing others who were tired and ready to get sober.

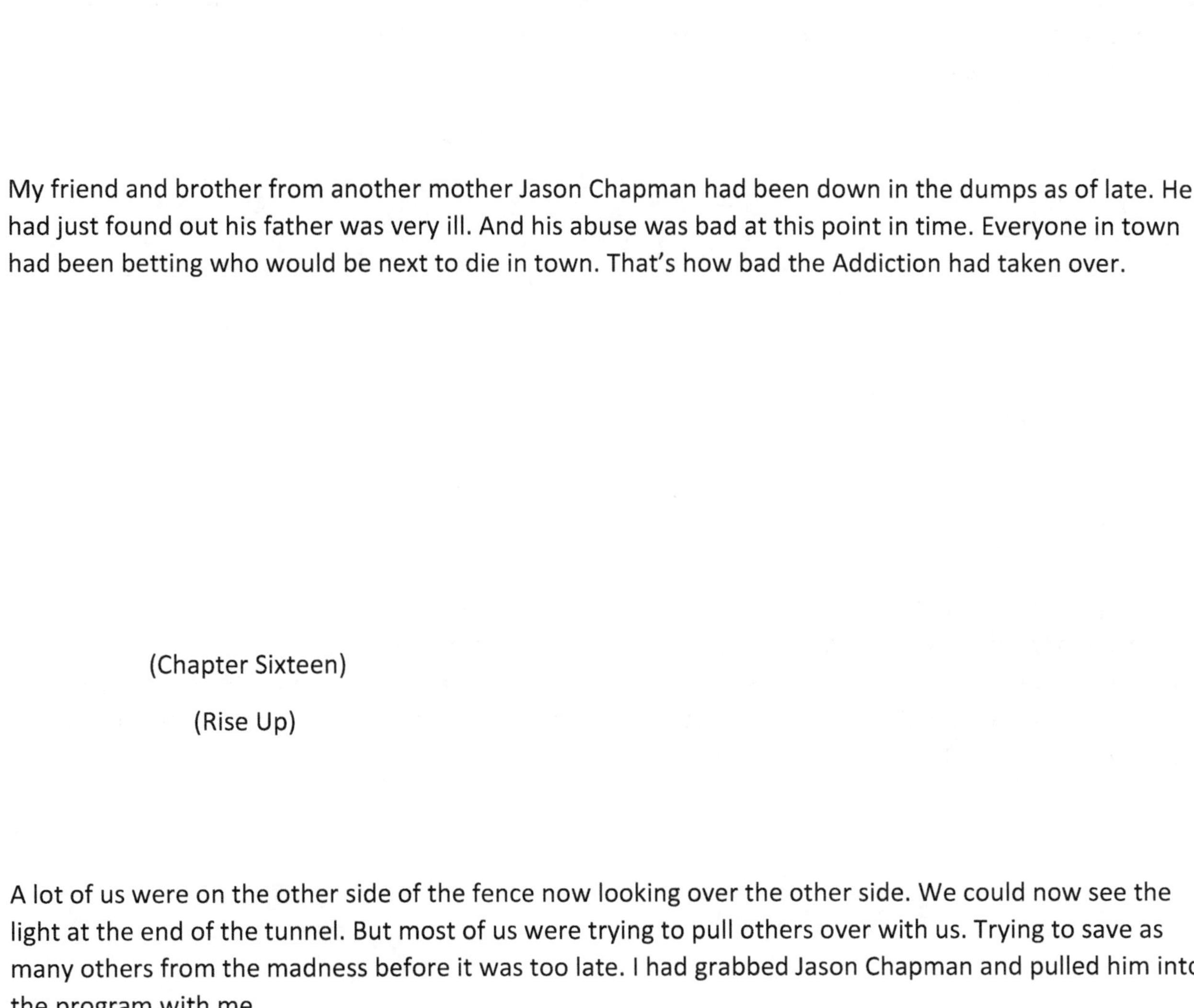

My friend and brother from another mother Jason Chapman had been down in the dumps as of late. He had just found out his father was very ill. And his abuse was bad at this point in time. Everyone in town had been betting who would be next to die in town. That's how bad the Addiction had taken over.

## (Chapter Sixteen)

## (Rise Up)

A lot of us were on the other side of the fence now looking over the other side. We could now see the light at the end of the tunnel. But most of us were trying to pull others over with us. Trying to save as many others from the madness before it was too late. I had grabbed Jason Chapman and pulled him into the program with me.

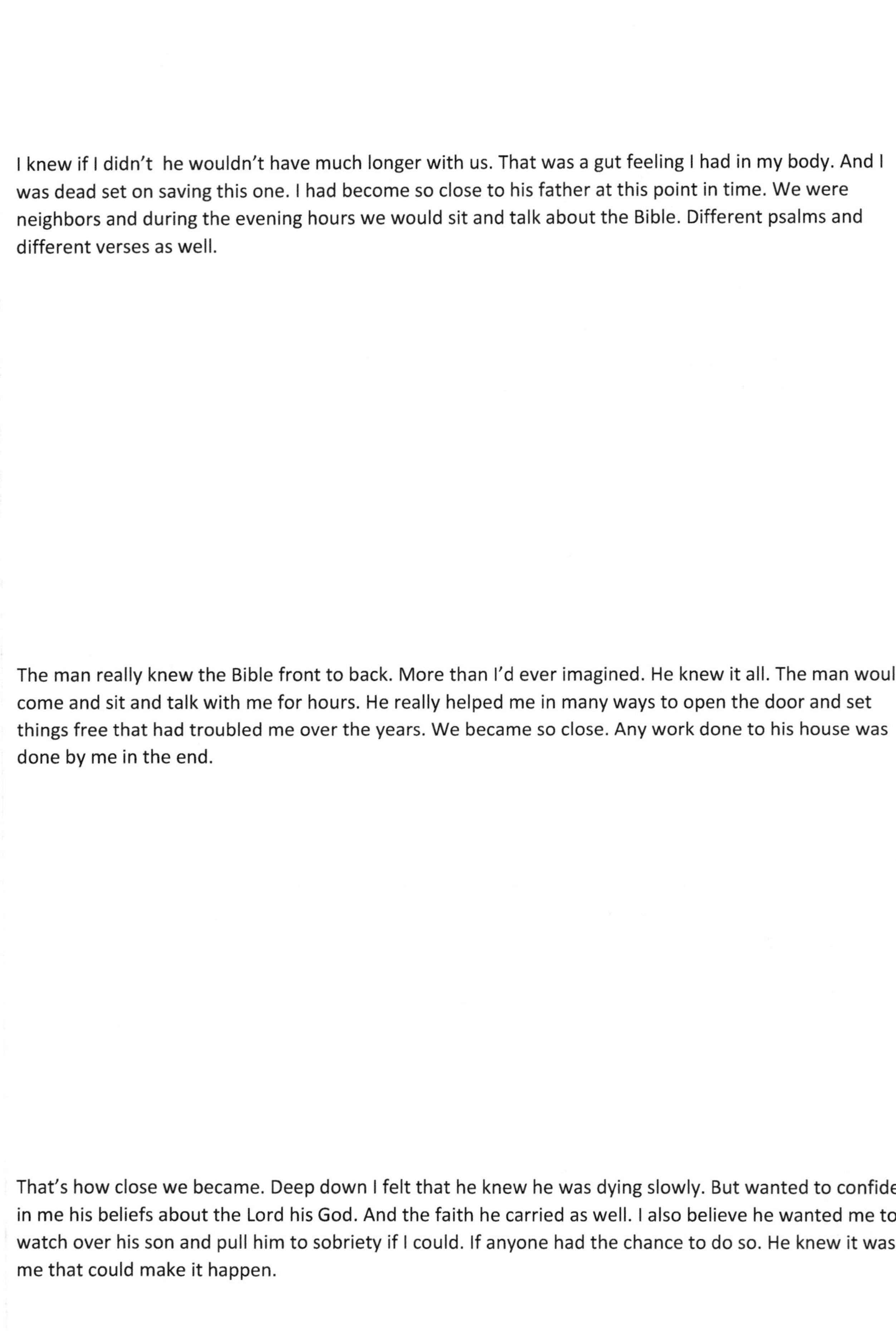

I knew if I didn't he wouldn't have much longer with us. That was a gut feeling I had in my body. And I was dead set on saving this one. I had become so close to his father at this point in time. We were neighbors and during the evening hours we would sit and talk about the Bible. Different psalms and different verses as well.

The man really knew the Bible front to back. More than I'd ever imagined. He knew it all. The man would come and sit and talk with me for hours. He really helped me in many ways to open the door and set things free that had troubled me over the years. We became so close. Any work done to his house was done by me in the end.

That's how close we became. Deep down I felt that he knew he was dying slowly. But wanted to confide in me his beliefs about the Lord his God. And the faith he carried as well. I also believe he wanted me to watch over his son and pull him to sobriety if I could. If anyone had the chance to do so. He knew it was me that could make it happen.

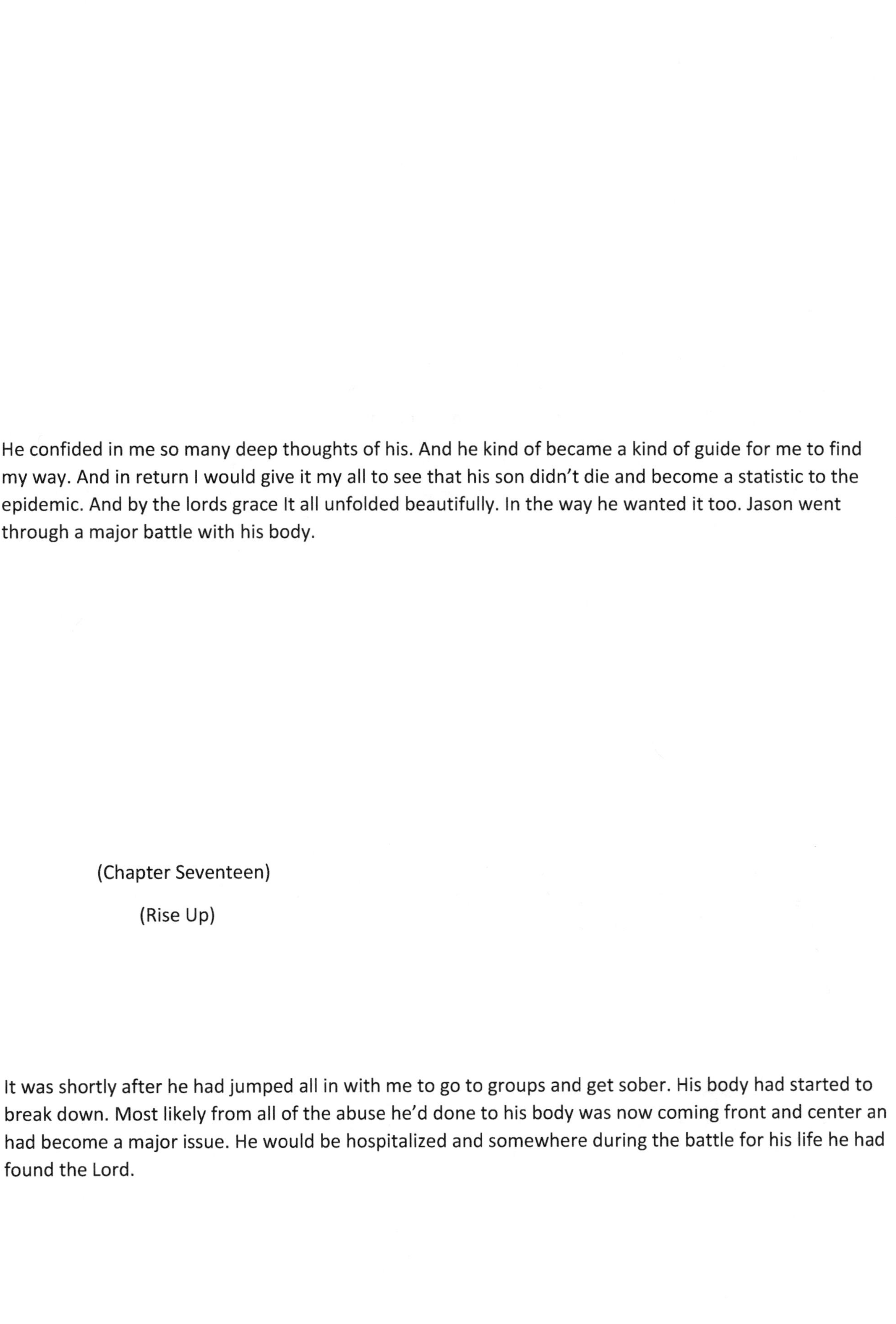

He confided in me so many deep thoughts of his. And he kind of became a kind of guide for me to find my way. And in return I would give it my all to see that his son didn't die and become a statistic to the epidemic. And by the lords grace It all unfolded beautifully. In the way he wanted it too. Jason went through a major battle with his body.

## (Chapter Seventeen)

## (Rise Up)

It was shortly after he had jumped all in with me to go to groups and get sober. His body had started to break down. Most likely from all of the abuse he'd done to his body was now coming front and center an had become a major issue. He would be hospitalized and somewhere during the battle for his life he had found the Lord.

And in that day it was all set in motion this young man would rise back up and take his life back. Before it had been to late to do so. And he started going to church every Sunday. He praised God every chance he could. He found his way finally and that made me happy as all ever. That I could be part of helping a friend a brother. To see the light and find his way.

After that Jason had found a good job. He saved up money and bought a new truck. The young man had found his groove. He was in the zone. And that alone made me feel so good. I know his father was looking down on him from heaven with a huge smile upon his face. The young man had put it all together.

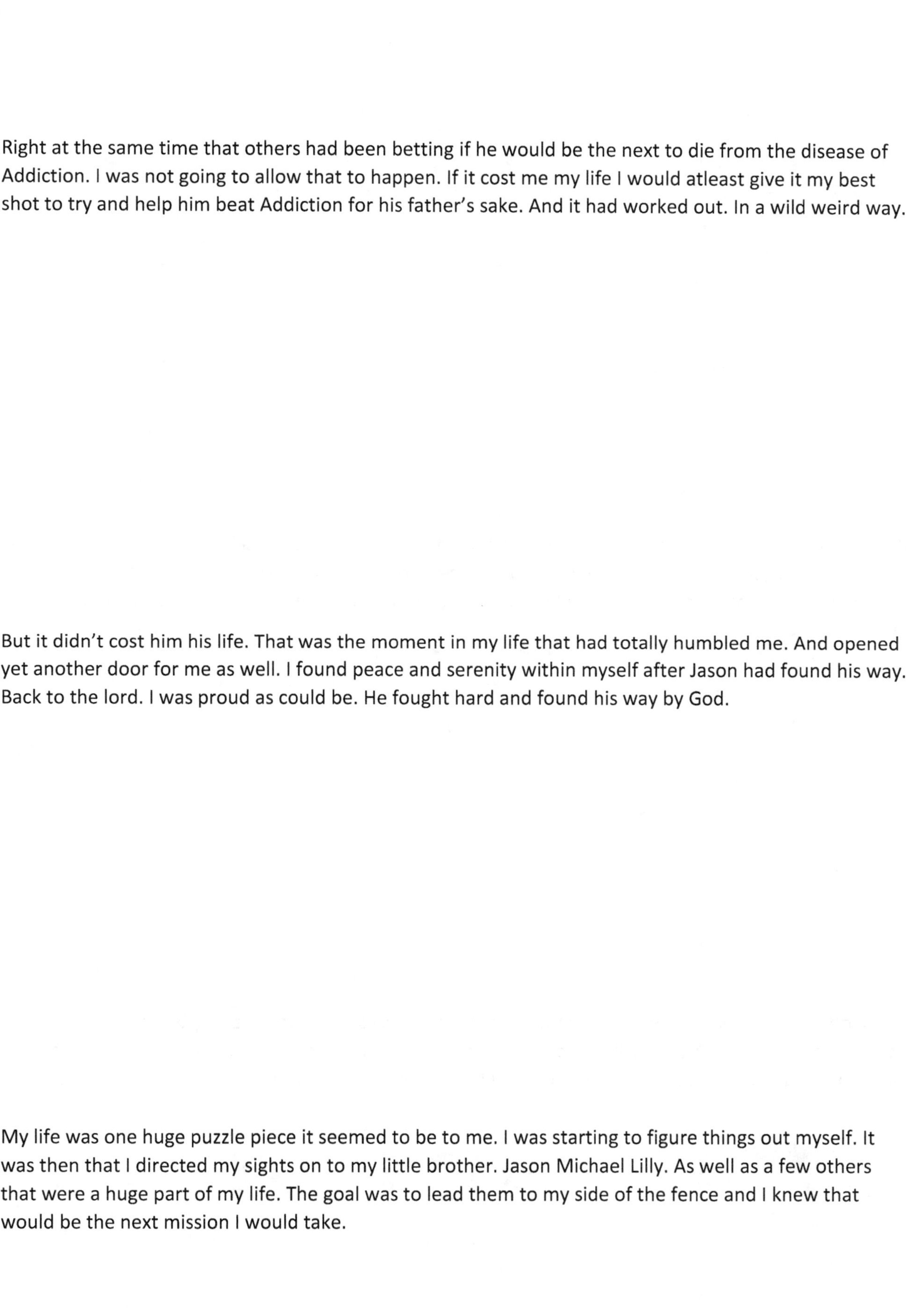

Right at the same time that others had been betting if he would be the next to die from the disease of Addiction. I was not going to allow that to happen. If it cost me my life I would atleast give it my best shot to try and help him beat Addiction for his father's sake. And it had worked out. In a wild weird way.

But it didn't cost him his life. That was the moment in my life that had totally humbled me. And opened yet another door for me as well. I found peace and serenity within myself after Jason had found his way. Back to the lord. I was proud as could be. He fought hard and found his way by God.

My life was one huge puzzle piece it seemed to be to me. I was starting to figure things out myself. It was then that I directed my sights on to my little brother. Jason Michael Lilly. As well as a few others that were a huge part of my life. The goal was to lead them to my side of the fence and I knew that would be the next mission I would take.

## (Chapter Eighteen)

## (Rise Up)

But what I didn't know was that I would not be able to help the situation at all. The course had been set and it was my brother's destiny in the end to go home to the lord. In the end he would lose his battle to Addiction. When I had just learned that he was struggling with it. To this point I had no clue that he was an addict.

He made sure it was kept a secret from me. All of his overdoses. The two times my brother Chad had used Narcan and saved his life. All kept a secret from me. By the time I would learn he was in trouble it would be to late. I think deep down about how I had found him that morning.

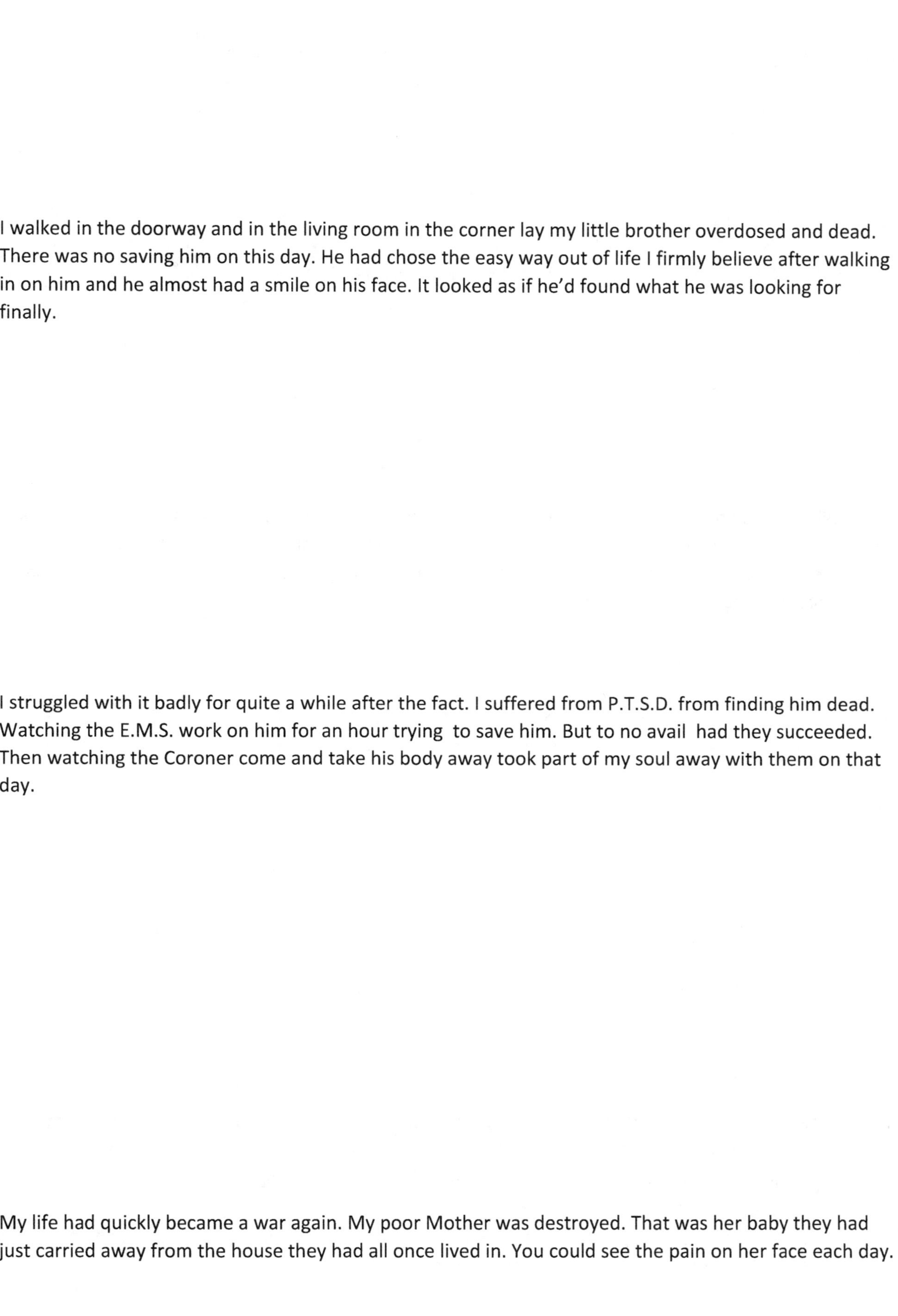

I walked in the doorway and in the living room in the corner lay my little brother overdosed and dead. There was no saving him on this day. He had chose the easy way out of life I firmly believe after walking in on him and he almost had a smile on his face. It looked as if he'd found what he was looking for finally.

I struggled with it badly for quite a while after the fact. I suffered from P.T.S.D. from finding him dead. Watching the E.M.S. work on him for an hour trying to save him. But to no avail had they succeeded. Then watching the Coroner come and take his body away took part of my soul away with them on that day.

My life had quickly became a war again. My poor Mother was destroyed. That was her baby they had just carried away from the house they had all once lived in. You could see the pain on her face each day.

Shortly after she was tested for Cancer the results had come back quickly. And she was diagnosed with Pancreatic Cancer.

As a family we tried to pull together in that moment. Unity was the most important word we could apply for this next battle. We had a family meeting shortly after. We knew that this would change things for us all. I and my Sisters Angie and Joanne would all move back home to help our Mother. We knew we had Months now not years left with her now.

## (Chapter Nineteen)

## (Rise Up)

Shortly after the meeting we would all plan on our moves back home. 3 months was now the Magic Number for our family. Once again another battle we would have to face. Our small town had lost so many loved ones at this point it had become traumatic. These were testing times for me.

I would find myself back in the reality of several drug lapses myself after the death of my little brother. At this moment I had just lost another loved one to Addiction. And had two others that I loved dearly battling Cancer. Ronnie had Cancer of the spine. And my Mother was battling Cancer of the Pancreas.

I had somehow allowed these situations to un ravel me. I had moved in with my mother akd was sleeping next to her on the floor during the night time hours. Keeping an eye on her constantly. She would struggle to hold a glass. She would most definitely struggle to get up and go to the bathroom as well.

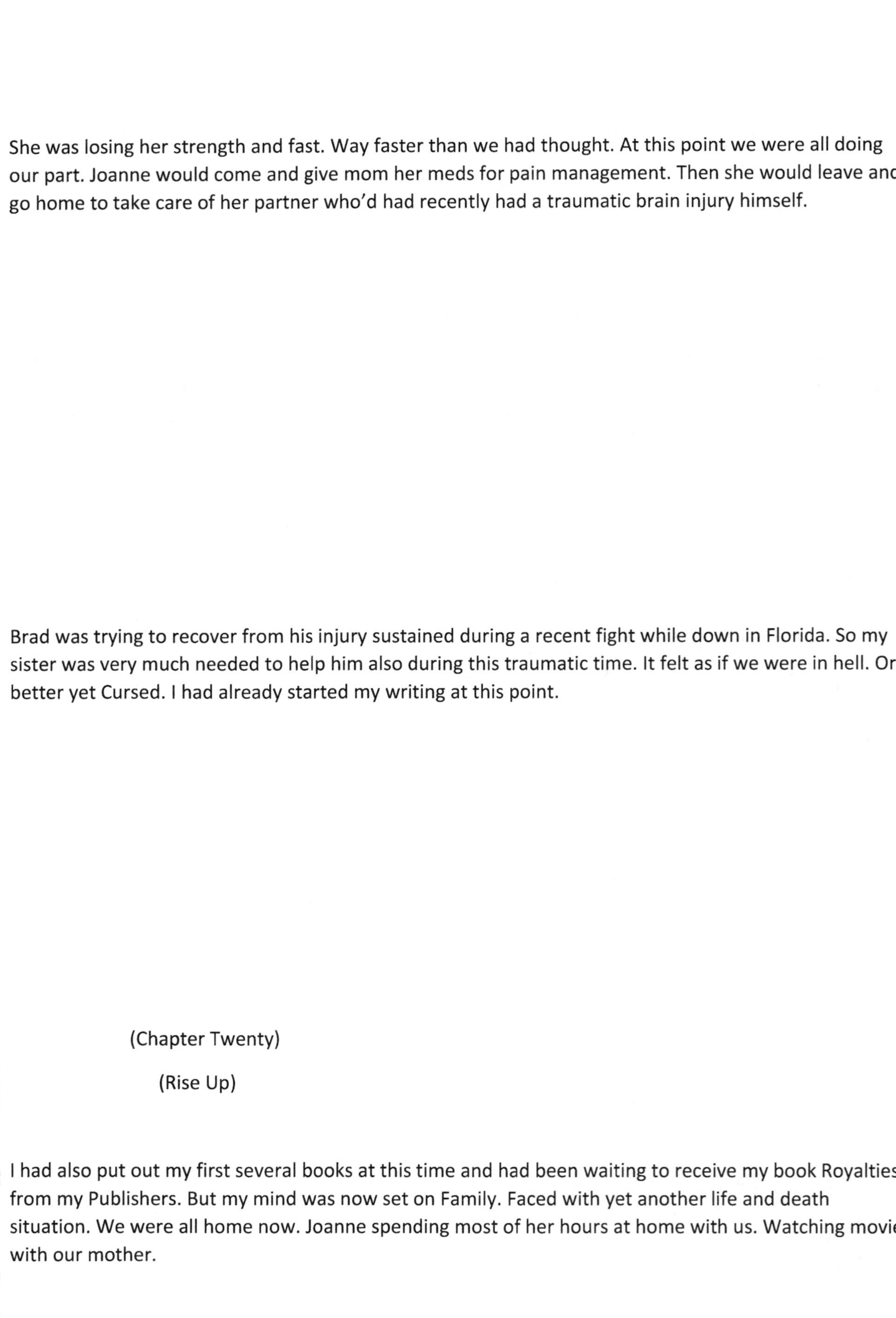

She was losing her strength and fast. Way faster than we had thought. At this point we were all doing our part. Joanne would come and give mom her meds for pain management. Then she would leave and go home to take care of her partner who'd had recently had a traumatic brain injury himself.

Brad was trying to recover from his injury sustained during a recent fight while down in Florida. So my sister was very much needed to help him also during this traumatic time. It felt as if we were in hell. Or better yet Cursed. I had already started my writing at this point.

## (Chapter Twenty)

### (Rise Up)

I had also put out my first several books at this time and had been waiting to receive my book Royalties from my Publishers. But my mind was now set on Family. Faced with yet another life and death situation. We were all home now. Joanne spending most of her hours at home with us. Watching movies with our mother.

Angie had also moved back home to help as much as she could. Taking care of our mother was like bitter sweet. It felt good to take care of the one who had taken care of us for so many years. But the situation was totally different she was seeing us grow and we were having to watch her slowly fade away from us.

Each day her strength would fade. We would be lucky to have her still with us by Christmas. It was Now Halloween night. Mom and Myself and Angie. Would give out candy to the kids on this night. Just as we did when we're were younger before leaving home. That feeling to was also bitter sweet.

We had been lucky to have another Holiday with mom. But would we get another. The test would be to make it to Thanksgiving. The nights with mom would become harder and longer and tougher. I awoke one night to being puked allover by my mother. She had eaten something earlier that night that had not settled with her well.

And she had awaken so sick she couldn't make it to the bathroom. It felt like the scene I had seen in many other horror movies. Up to this point in all of my families lives. All that we seemed to deal with anymore was tragedy and death of lived ones. It had all started once we had lost Grandma Hazel and Papaw Luke.

## (Chapter Twenty One)

## (Rise Up)

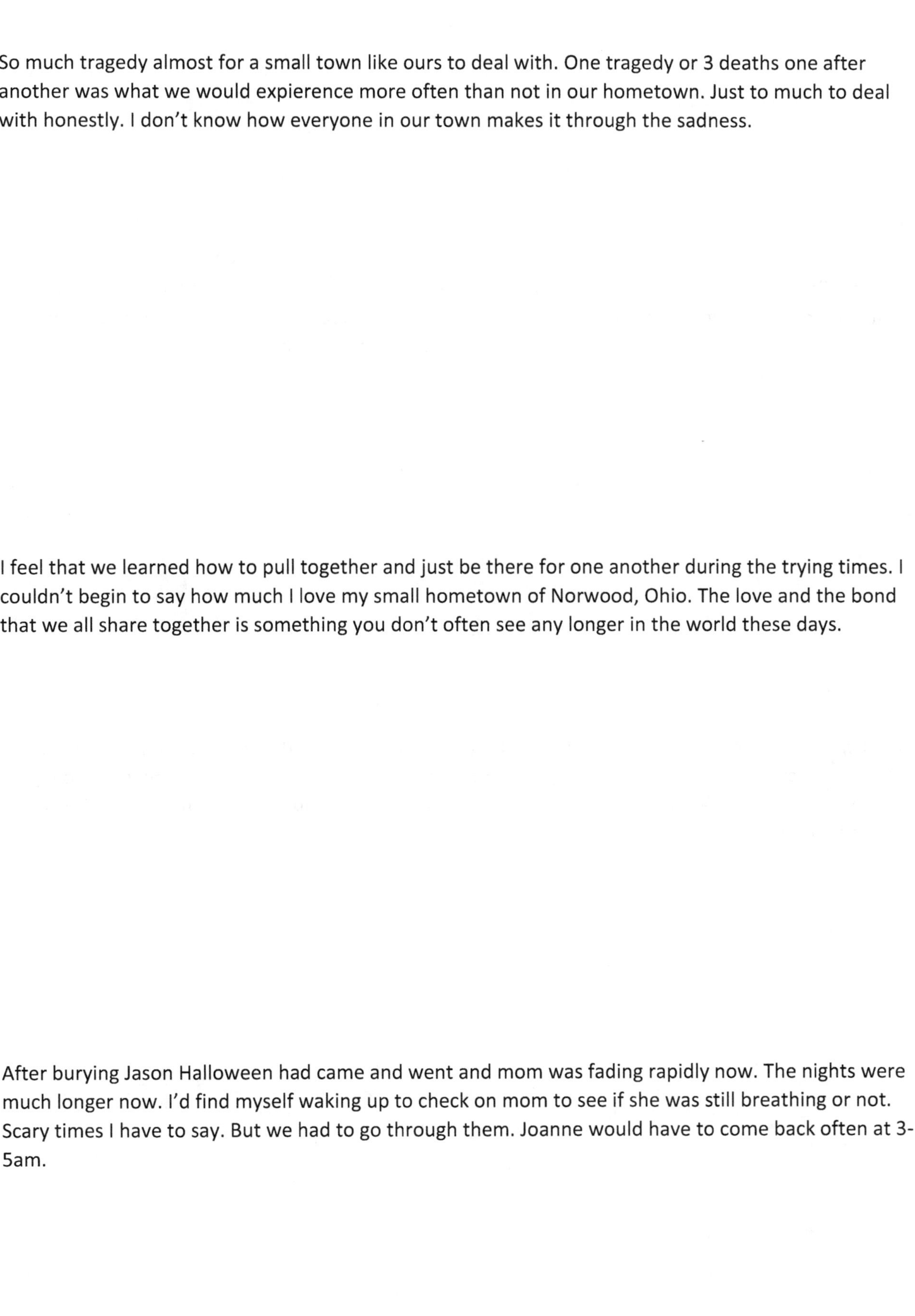

So much tragedy almost for a small town like ours to deal with. One tragedy or 3 deaths one after another was what we would expierence more often than not in our hometown. Just to much to deal with honestly. I don't know how everyone in our town makes it through the sadness.

I feel that we learned how to pull together and just be there for one another during the trying times. I couldn't begin to say how much I love my small hometown of Norwood, Ohio. The love and the bond that we all share together is something you don't often see any longer in the world these days.

After burying Jason Halloween had came and went and mom was fading rapidly now. The nights were much longer now. I'd find myself waking up to check on mom to see if she was still breathing or not. Scary times I have to say. But we had to go through them. Joanne would have to come back often at 3-5am.

The pain pills had started to become weak to the pain mom was now suffering. We got with the doctor and nurses and set a plan in motion to get a new mixture going to relieve moms pain levels. Once we had done that she was way more comfortable than she was just hours before hand.

At least we had pulled together a plan to get her pain levels fixed. Now the goal was to try and make it to Christmas Day. This would be a blessing if it happened. We had so many visitors coming and going at this point it was insane. So many people loved this woman. She had touched so many hearts with her kindness for others.

## (Chapter Twenty Two)

## (Rise Up)

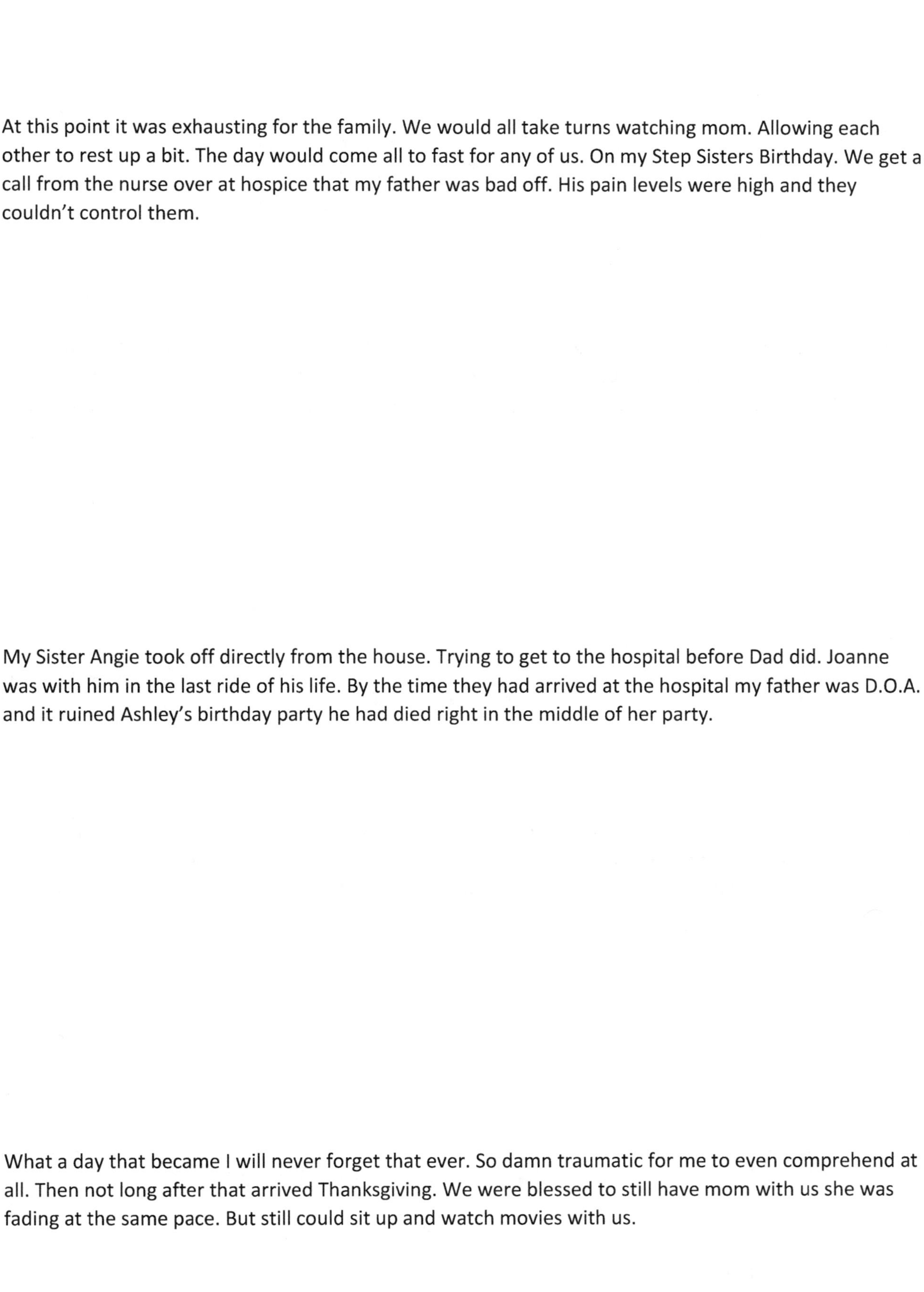

At this point it was exhausting for the family. We would all take turns watching mom. Allowing each other to rest up a bit. The day would come all to fast for any of us. On my Step Sisters Birthday. We get a call from the nurse over at hospice that my father was bad off. His pain levels were high and they couldn't control them.

My Sister Angie took off directly from the house. Trying to get to the hospital before Dad did. Joanne was with him in the last ride of his life. By the time they had arrived at the hospital my father was D.O.A. and it ruined Ashley's birthday party he had died right in the middle of her party.

What a day that became I will never forget that ever. So damn traumatic for me to even comprehend at all. Then not long after that arrived Thanksgiving. We were blessed to still have mom with us she was fading at the same pace. But still could sit up and watch movies with us.

We had the whole family with us during this Holiday we knew it may be the last one with our Mother among us. Thanksgiving went well because we were all together as a whole family. It felt so good everyone home and eating together as a family a unit. I felt so humbled that the lord had allowed us to have mom still.

Now could we make it until Christmas. Would the lord allow it that was my biggest worry of all as I sat and watched everyone sit and eat with mom that night. It was a great night. The feeling was so calm. Everyone home together and getting along. Watching movies the family all together for the first time in years.

(Chapter Twenty Three)

(Rise Up)

Everyone stayed late Thanksgiving night. Spent as much time as they could with mom before going home. Noone really wanted to leave her when they did. But life had to move forward. Lives had to be lived and the night ended with a highlight of love and plenty of hugs and kisses and I love you being spoken.

The weeks that transpired after Thanksgiving were way worse. One after the next mom just fell apart. Shortly before Christmas we awoke and mom was unchanged. She had slipped into a state of a coma just the day before. And was not coming out of it.

The situation was changing by the hour. Worse and worse she was becoming and the pain even worse. We could see the pain on her face at this point. Changing all of the time it seemed. It was December 23rd and we were so close to Christmas now. But it didn't seem like she was going to make it. The nurse came and said it was time for hospice care.

Mom had been so tough to make it at home all of the time that she had. But with her being at hospice she would receive the medicine to make her comfortable as she slowly left us. The Ambulance was on its way as we all kissed our mother and told her goodbye. We knew we'd never see her alive again after today.

And that was so damn tough on me. After the a balance had came and took her away. I remember calling my go to guy and buying a bunch of Xanax which weren't really Xanax. They were Fentanyl pills. I wanted to get tore up from the floor up at this point in time. I was now so beside myself. I didn't care what sobriety was.

After he came I took them immediately and shortly after was in my own little world without pain. But I still had my mom weighing heavily on my mind. She was fighting to stay alive I knew that much still. She had fought to make it the short amount of time that she'd had already.

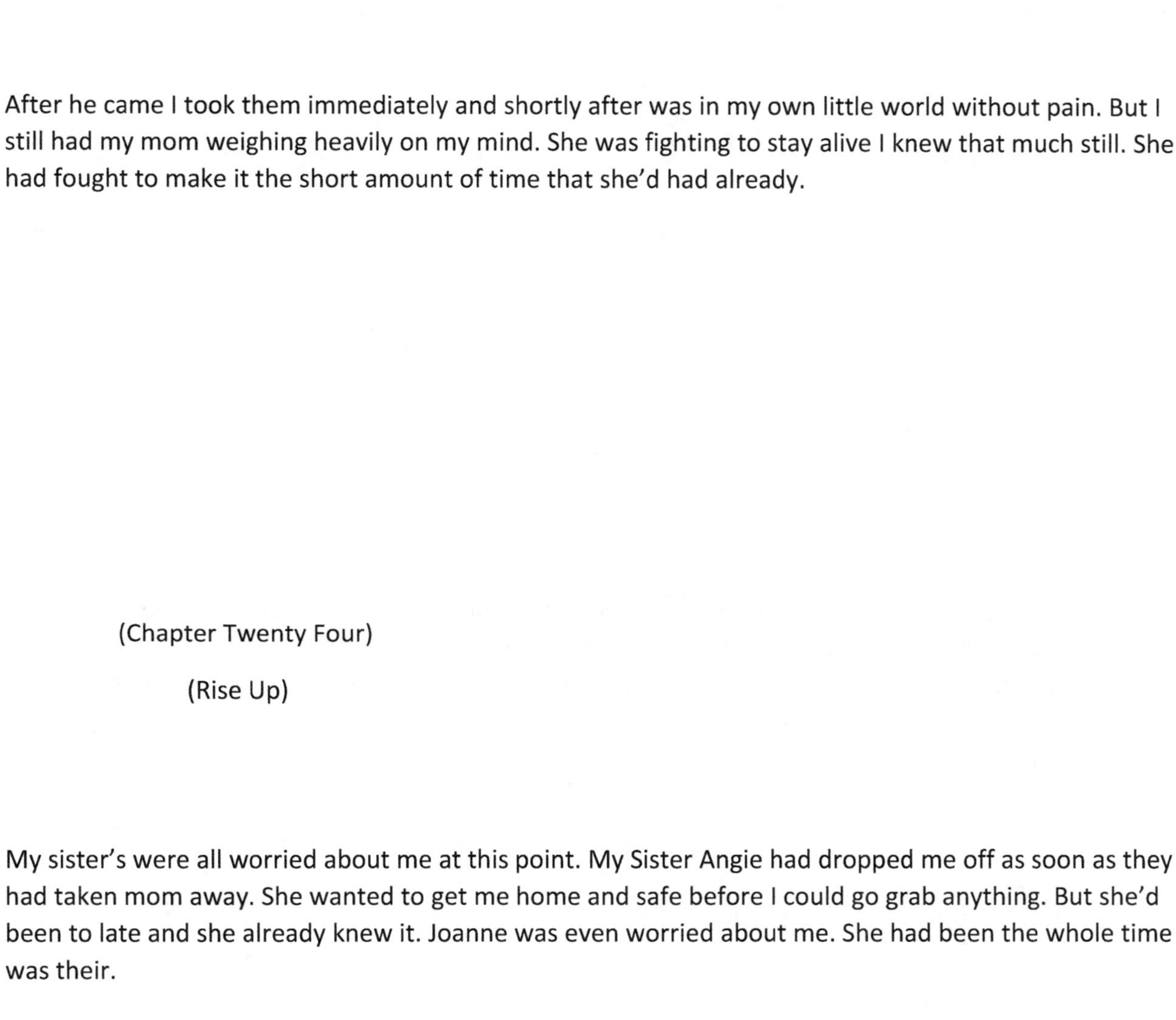

## (Chapter Twenty Four)

## (Rise Up)

My sister's were all worried about me at this point. My Sister Angie had dropped me off as soon as they had taken mom away. She wanted to get me home and safe before I could go grab anything. But she'd been to late and she already knew it. Joanne was even worried about me. She had been the whole time I was their.

Worried about me being in Norwood where it was super dangerous for me to be at anytime. Especially during times like this. We had just lost Jason and Dad and Mom now was coming sooner than later. She was well on her way out now. I knew that they would get her there and medicate her heavily enough for her to be out of pain.

The fact that we were losing her was what was killing me. I couldn't understand why God was taking all of our loved ones the way that he was. It just seemed to be way to many all at once for me to accept. I knew I had no choice but to accept it. And I'd better do so quickly. Because it was coming and fast.

I arrived back at home which in the moment made me happy. But I knew it was coming with another loss behind it. I had fought so hard to get so damn far but just couldn't seem to get over that final hump. To get to the other side of the fortune and fame realm. I had worked so hard and had written so much. I'd had over 25 books done at that point.

And only a couple of them had made me some money. My first two books had been doing descent but the release of my other books was taking place. I was working on several projects at a time. I was doing kids books as well as adult books as well. Even doing some new projects. I was now working on a new Zombie Series called The Zombie Stalkers.

Shortly after waking up on the morning of Christmas. I recieved a call from my Sister. She said that mom had been incoherent since the day she'd arrived at hospice. And she didn't have much longer now. We really didn't celebrate the holiday. We celebrated the birth of Christ our father but that was pretty much it.

She passed away on the 28th. Making it passed the holiday. Even though she'd suffered she made it through Christmas. I was glad for that fact that was all that mattered to me. I was glad for the time I had been given with my mother. We buried her a week later and my life changed all together.

## (Chapter Twenty Five)

## (Rise Up)

I had just completed a couple of serious projects on my own now. My 1st publisher was so busy at this point with a new Author who had suffered some tragedy as well. So I figured I'd go on my own for a while and do some things myself. By may of 2022 I was well on my way with over 50 books that had been written. Some better than others. But all in all I had grown as a writer.

I had a few books that were doing well at the moment. Some in sales of Paperback form. And coming in by way of the Kindle reading app as well. I figured that a few of my projects would have taken off a little bit better than they actually did. But I was only in my 2nd year of writing. I was expecting way too much to fast.

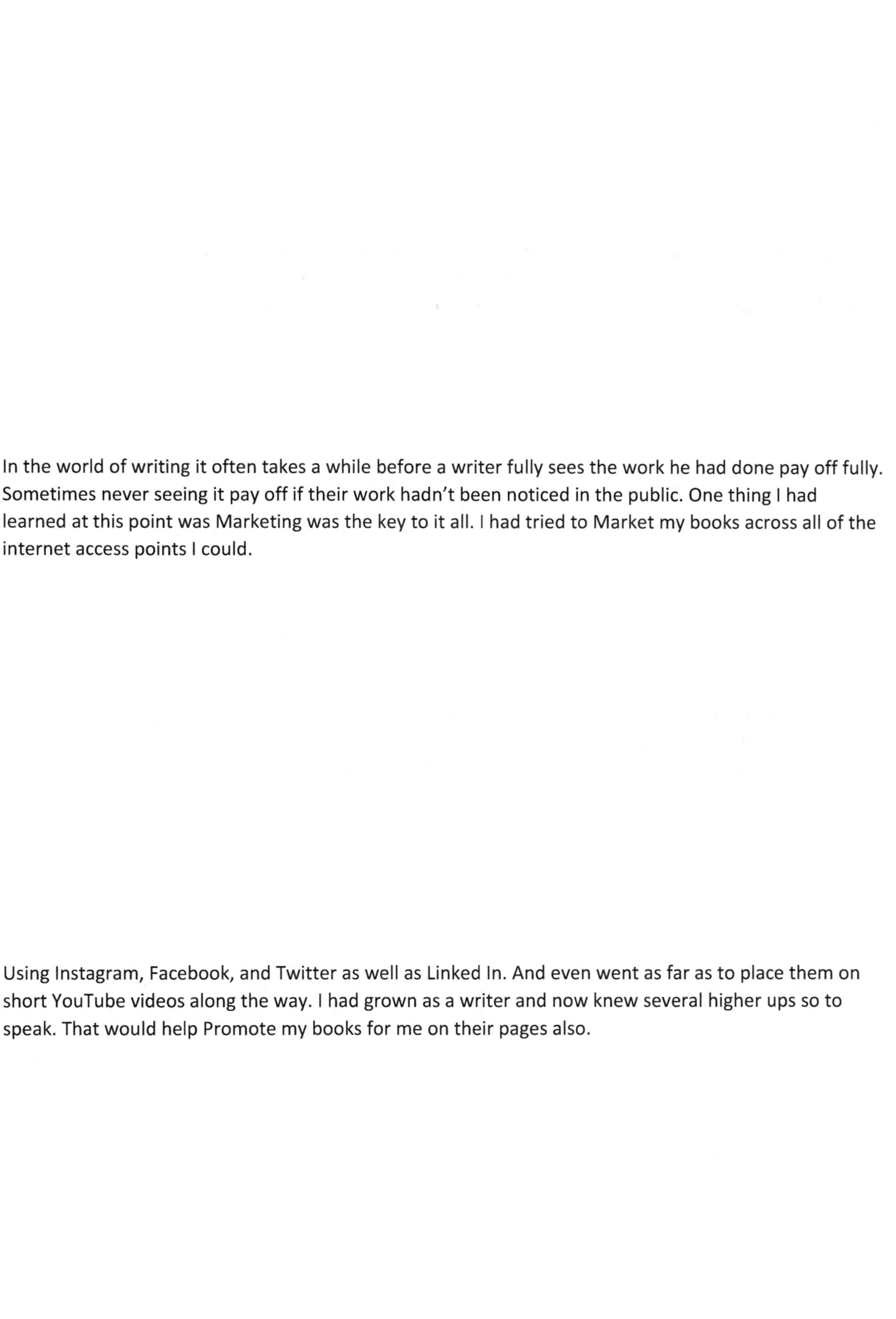

In the world of writing it often takes a while before a writer fully sees the work he had done pay off fully. Sometimes never seeing it pay off if their work hadn't been noticed in the public. One thing I had learned at this point was Marketing was the key to it all. I had tried to Market my books across all of the internet access points I could.

Using Instagram, Facebook, and Twitter as well as Linked In. And even went as far as to place them on short YouTube videos along the way. I had grown as a writer and now knew several higher ups so to speak. That would help Promote my books for me on their pages also.

I now had a total of 8 books at the local Library of Cincinnati and the surrounding towns as well. The goal was Ten and I was close. Only 2 books away by 2022 my 2nd year of writing. In my heart and soul I was feeling like if I had to write 500 books to get their I would. I wanted to live a different t life before I left this world.

The kind of life where I wouldn't have to suffer or struggle any longer. I had the motivation and the will power to make it happen. Nothing was going to break me. I had many ideas flowing and was thinking at this point to stretch my latest book series up to a total of ten maybe 15 before ending it

## (Chapter Twenty Six)

## (Rise Up)

The series itself was doing well at the library. Each of them being checked out on a regular basis. People seemed to like my writing very much in my hometown. I kept a watch on just how well my books were doing at the library as well as in sales and on kindle also. I was far from finished that was for sure. In my mind I was going to speak it all into existence.

I wasn't going to allow myself to fail. Even though honestly I had succeeded very well. Just having one book at the library was a huge accomplishment. I almost had ten sitting on the shelves now. I had a lot to be proud of. Even though I had still not received any of my royalties from Amazon as of yet.

I knew it would come together sooner now than later. I had made all of the necessary adjustments to my bank account to complete the transactions. I was just waiting for my upgraded card now to come in the mail any day now. And when that finally happened maybe just maybe I could start making my rise up into a different way of living finally.

I had a few more ideas now stewing up inside of my head now. Upon the completion of my last book I would take the series itself to the next level. Exciting the readers and keeping them tuned in to the whole book. My goal as a writer was to keep the reader interested the whole time. From start to finish of each book I'd written.

Everything was now set in place finally for me to take off as an Author. I was now thinking of new ideas for new titles. New stories to write about. My mind was growing as a writer now. But I had encountered more financial troubles once again. It seemed as if every time I rose up to the occasion something else would knock me back down.

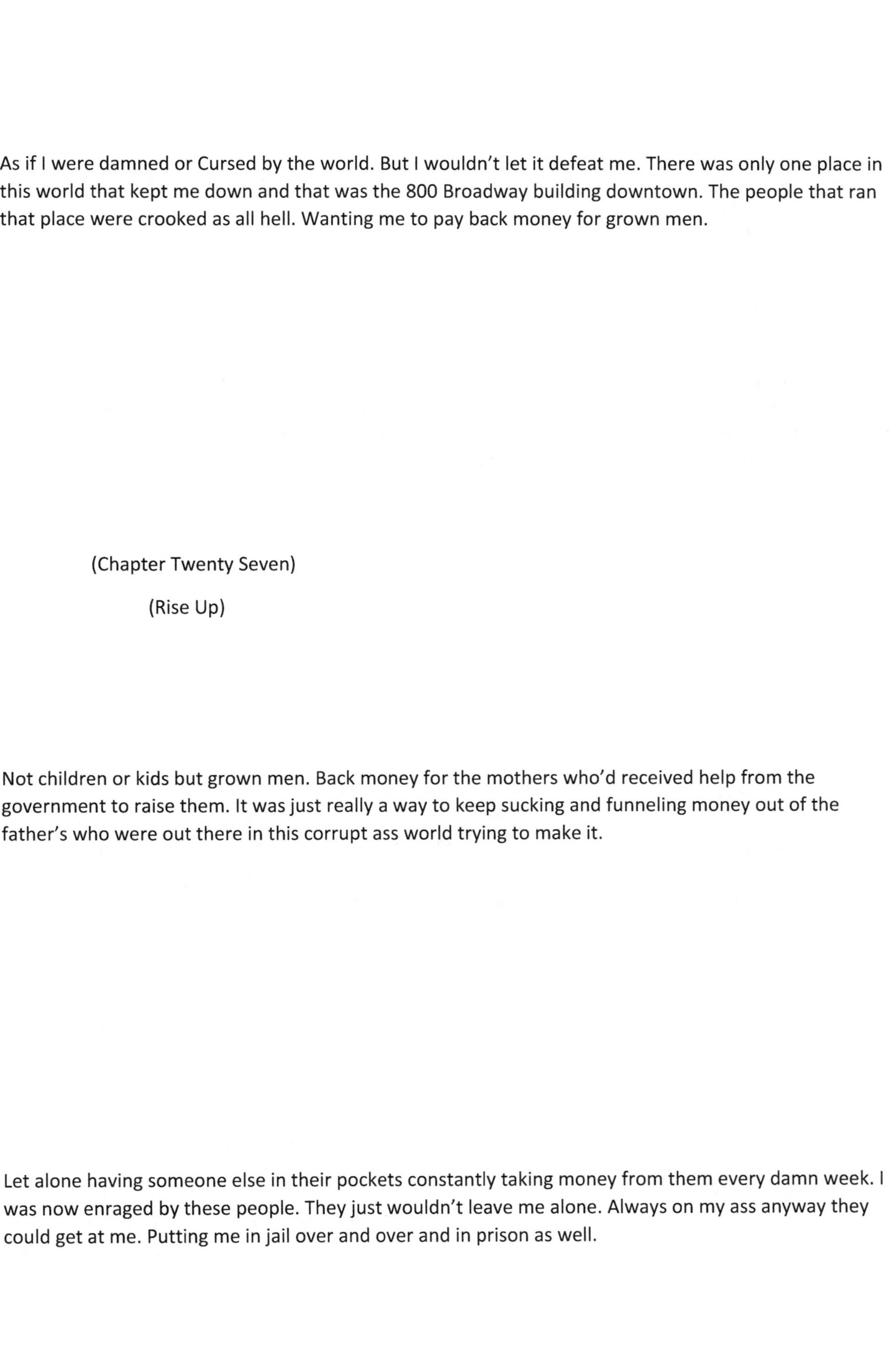

As if I were damned or Cursed by the world. But I wouldn't let it defeat me. There was only one place in this world that kept me down and that was the 800 Broadway building downtown. The people that ran that place were crooked as all hell. Wanting me to pay back money for grown men.

## (Chapter Twenty Seven)

### (Rise Up)

Not children or kids but grown men. Back money for the mothers who'd received help from the government to raise them. It was just really a way to keep sucking and funneling money out of the father's who were out there in this corrupt ass world trying to make it.

Let alone having someone else in their pockets constantly taking money from them every damn week. I was now enraged by these people. They just wouldn't leave me alone. Always on my ass anyway they could get at me. Putting me in jail over and over and in prison as well.

And we're waiting at the gates for me when I got released and re arrested me again for the same charge. Which was against the damn law in all honesty. I've been harassed and bombarded by these people over and over. And as soon as I hit the ranks of Author. Here they come at me yet once again. Acting as if I owe a total of 500,000 dollars for back support which is totally wrong.

Trying  to take money from my paycheck as well as my book royalties. Threatening if I didn't give them access to my sales from my books that they would just lock me up. I've seen that game already being hit the 30 day deal in jail. Then 60 days and then 90 days also and then 3 years in prison. Then they start it all over again.

The whole system needs to be looked over in all honesty. I'm not going to allow this world to consume me. I am a man of faith. I will not allow myself to he broken by the system. I have come down to many roads of doom. I have witnessed to much pain and death and wickedness in my days. I feel I've finally earned the right to live a better life for once.

## (Chapter Twenty Eight)

## ( Rise Up)

But he'll who am I to say what I've earned. All of the power is held by our lord our savior and I will just keep my faith in knowing he has the plans set in motion for me. And with that being said I will just continue down my road of travel learning from each choice made and every error that I make as well striving to be a better person.

But I will be damned if I allow myself to be strong armed by anyone. No matter what the sentence. I will go through the hell and once it is over. I will know that I can move forward with the plans I have set in place upon my release from that hell hole. See I'm writing this knowing of what's going to happen to me in the near future.

They will jail me coming real soon. And I will be left without my medicine which is prescribed to me by my family doctor. They will make me suffer and go through withdrawals. Deprive me of any satisfaction of any kind. For 21 days I will go through pure hell. And if I'm lucky I Will make it home once again.

To set my career in motion once again if lucky enough. Everything I'm tested by evil I always prevail. Never giving up never losing focus on my faith in God. That is the key through all of life's situations. Once you lose your faith you lose it all. So never lose the faith ever in life.

(Chapter Twenty Nine)

(Rise Up)

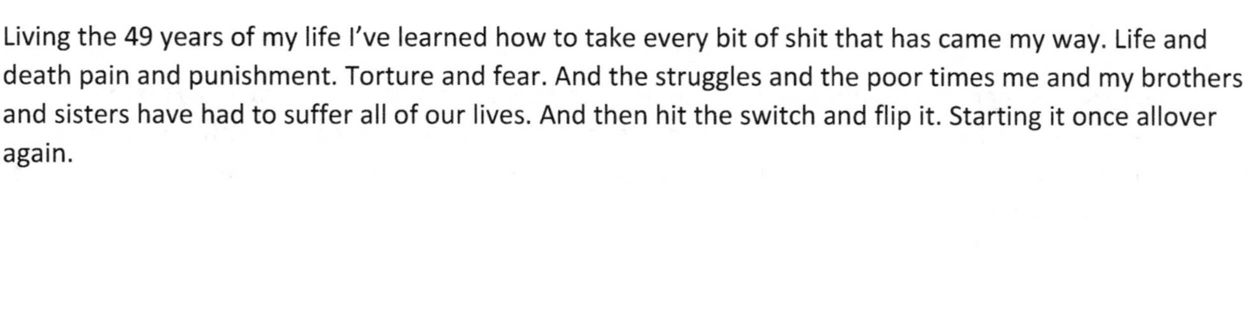

Living the 49 years of my life I've learned how to take every bit of shit that has came my way. Life and death pain and punishment. Torture and fear. And the struggles and the poor times me and my brothers and sisters have had to suffer all of our lives. And then hit the switch and flip it. Starting it once allover again.

That's been my life's tests over and over again. Day after day. Month after month and year after year. The Devil hoping that I would break down along some where along the way. Which I did as a young vulnerable kid. But as a man who found his way through all of that hell I was put through was not enough.

I was also stabbed a total of 7 times as well to deal with that pain for a while. Being forced to suffer being given the worst and weakest of medicines for not telling on the individual who'd actually stabbed me. I've been rock solid all the way. I've saved lives when the evil around me was wanting me to just take them instead.

I as a man have learned to live with a whole lot of hurt and pain and mental anguish in my lifetime. Never breaking down fully. If anyone deserves the right to live out their last days months or years on this earth. I feel that I have earned that right finally as I said before. But only the lord God above will set those plans in motion when the time comes.

## (Chapter Thirty)

## (Rise)

The things I've have seen the things I have gone through in life have raised me to be an overall better man towards the later years of my life. I've always been a kind and loving individual. But in my later years did I learn to deeply love and help others when in need.

And I then tried to show others how to turn that anger and pain into something else. Changing their lives by restoring their faith in God life and humanity. As grim as it looks at this time. With the horrible leaders that we now have ruling over our country. It really looks horrible our future.

The prices of food and building materials and fuel are at an overall high as ever seen before. Showing us just why the ones who ended up in office wanted to be their in the first place. It's grown to be all about lining your own pockets by doing back door deals along the way.

We had the one we needed in office and they made sure he was ousted by playing dirty games and dirty politics. And now I fear for this world more than I ever have. I worry about our children and grand children's future's. Wondering will they have what they need. Will they be given a fair shake in life.

I know one thing if they are part of my family they will be just fine. Because we were all raised and taught to not break ever. Regardless of what we've Been put through no matter how bad it is to push forward through it. To rock up and move on forward from that moment in time.

## (Chapter Thirty One)

## (Rise Up)

Rise above it all that is how I was raised and learned in due time how to overcome all of my life's obstacles one after the other. And let me say this I've had well more than my fair share in life and there is no doubt at all about that. Years and years of struggling g and seeing everyone else around you doing the same damn thing.

Rising back up off of the ground only to get back up on the horse. To be knocked right back off of it and yet get up over and over again. Never allowing yourself to just give up. It is in those moments that you define who you are and what kind of family that you really come from.

And earning the love and respect from so many others around you along the way. That is how I've lived my whole life. Time and time again. Getting back up when knocked down by the hell and the chaos that constantly followed me around my whole life's journey.

In the end I would have to say that all of the hell and turmoil I and others I've had the privilege knowing has given me the strength to always push forward through any hellish moments I may have to go through in my lifetime. Each person played a key role in the making of me becoming a better man along my journey.

I am so proud to have known each and every single person I have known. They have all taught me so much about life. So many of them are gone now. God taking them away from me way to early. I won't question his actions at all. He lay's plans out for us along our way. I guess we pay for our choices along the way.

The right ones take us up a ways on the ladder and the wrong ones take us down a couple of notches. I've tried as I've become an older man now to male the right choices in each and every single move I make along the way in life. I've came a very long way in my lifetime. I've battled through so many situations.

But all it does is make me continue to grow as a person as well as a man. Learning from all of the mistakes we make is what matters most in life. If we don't learn from it how can we move forward or grow into a better person. That's what mistakes are all about so we can learn how to Rise up above it all.

(The End)

(Written By Jeffrey Lilly)

(May 10th 2022)

This book is dedicated to all of those we have lost in Addiction as well as life's tragedies. Changing our lives along the way as we learn to become better human beings.

www.ingramcontent.com/pod-product-compliance
Lightning Source LLC
LaVergne TN
LVHW080556160826
845677LV00010B/1875
* 9 7 9 8 8 2 4 8 9 6 6 5 7 *